COUNTDOWN
to
love

About the Authors

David Matchmaker Hinds (yes, this is his real name and he has heard all the jokes) is an award-winning stress management consultant and relationships adviser who has inspired tens of thousands of people with his seminars, hospital tours and health books. He is the best-selling author of *After Stroke* (with a foreword by Sir Peter Morris, Nuffield Professor of Surgery at the University of Oxford, published in the UK and USA by Thorsons and in Japan by Sunchoh Shuppan). Other recent titles include *Beat Depression* (Hodder and Stoughton, Arabic edition by Jarir of Saudi Arabia) and *The Little Book of Recovery* (CHP).

David's books have featured extensively on UK national television, including two documentary series, *This Morning* on ITV and *Five News,* as well as being favourably reviewed in the national press and colour magazines. Few people possess the insight that comes from a career of listening and responding to the problems of managing stress, crises and relationships. Fewer still, the tenacity and expertise to take readers to the core of their ability to create and enhance a loving relationship with the person who is right for them.

Tatiana Hinds, David's wife and co-author, researched and devised the Matchmaking Equation that is at the very heart of *Countdown to Love:* a measured and reliable system for estimating human compatibility and the likelihood of two people enjoying a happy and lasting relationship together. She graduated from university in Moscow with a first class honours degree and is currently specialising in relationship statistics. In addition to being a UK-qualified teacher of mathematics working full-time for the local education authority in Cornwall, Tatiana co-hosts Countdown seminars and workshops with David.

The authors are happily married and live in the idyllic fishing village of Polperro. David and Tatiana's deep understanding of the mix of factors that evolve to make relationships work uniquely qualifies them as love coaches. Their warmth, passion and commitment to the Countdown project will inspire and enable present and future generations to be happy in love.

David & Tatiana Hinds

COUNTDOWN
to
love

find your ideal partner
this time for good

foulsham
LONDON • NEW YORK • TORONTO • SYDNEY

foulsham

The Publishing House, Bennetts Close, Cippenham, Slough,
Berkshire, SL1 5AP, England

Foulsham books can be found in all good bookshops or direct from
www.foulsham.com

ISBN 0-572-03149-1

Cover silhouette by Alamy B/G

A CIP record for this book is available from the British Library.

The moral right of the author has been asserted

Printed in Great Britain by Mackays of Chatham Ltd, Chatham, Kent

CONTENTS

ACKNOWLEDGEMENTS

We are immensely grateful to Richard Madeley and Judy Finnigan, Jilly and Leo Cooper, Neil and Glenys Kinnock, Archbishop George and Lady Carey, Neil and Christine Hamilton, John Dankworth and Cleo Laine for their contributions.

Special thanks to everyone at Foulsham who has worked tirelessly to bring Countdown to life. In particular, we are indebted to Wendy Hobson for her encouragement during the writing process; Julia Thorley who edited the manuscript so skilfully; Emma Hamilton for making the editorial process seem so natural; Roger Hammond, for his stunning cover design; Deborah Murray who designed the text; Chris Brewer, for his typesetting expertise; Holly Belasco and Margaret Lashbrook for their outstanding PR and marketing expertise; and Barry Belasco whose hands-on approach, attention to detail and belief in the book are the stuff of authors' dreams.

Our long-suffering friends in different parts of the world (and, in many instances, their partners, their exes, and their exes' ex!) warrant confidential but significant recognition for allowing us to test and retest the quality of their relationships during the development and fine-tuning stages of the Matchmaking Equation.

Finally, well-deserved praise to the Countdown team for their untiring efforts, irrepressible enthusiasm and sheer genius in delivering life-changing events to people of all ages in the space of one short weekend. Derek Campbell – we couldn't have done it without you – you are our guiding star and quality control department all wrapped into one. Gillie Scherr, Chris Stephens and the entire back-up team in Plymouth – we couldn't stage these extravaganzas without your phenomenal *behind the scenes* contribution. Adrian Bold, Steve Davey, Richard Simeons and Gloria Payge – you came into our busy lives at just the right moment and your input has been of crucial importance. You are the unsung heroes and heroines of our success.

Thank you for helping us to bring about this great adventure called *Countdown to Love*.

FOREWORD

After the honeymoon, when Tatiana and I settled down to married life in Cornwall, we discovered that neither of us was accustomed to cooking or washing up. During our courting years in London, Moscow and the West Country, we had eaten in local restaurants, enjoyed takeaways or been treated by mothers, sisters, nieces or friends. Before that, Tatiana had always lived at home with mum and dinner was something that turned up whenever she was hungry. For my part, with six pubs in the village all serving good food, I thought the kitchen made the ideal walk-in filing cabinet.

From that inauspicious start, we devised a system of work sharing that suits us both. During the week, Tatiana is kitchen person; at the weekends, I masquerade as the resident chef, butler and washer-upper, pandering to her every culinary whim. If you think that arrangement is a little one-sided, you'll love our arrangements for completing this book!

I burn the midnight oil doing all the drafting (which is why I write in the first person throughout the narrative) and she does what she does best – sitting in a hot, perfumed bath devising and testing matchmaking equations to her heart's content. *Isn't this what all mathematicians do?* I used to ask myself. Not any more! Having marvelled at the accuracy and ease-of-use with which the longevity of a relationship can be predicted by the Matchmaking Equation she has created for *Countdown to Love,* I consider my contribution the easy bit.

David M Hinds, Polperro, England

INTRODUCTION

Why do some people find their ideal partner while others stagger from one broken relationship to the next or live their life alone? What enables some couples to have loving relationships that last while others end up on the rocks? And why do so many people who are unlucky in love keep choosing the same type of person?

How many truly loving couples of your own generation do you know with a long-term record of togetherness, partnerships that are admired by friends and strangers for the richness and humanity of their affection for each other?

Do these magnificent twosomes possess outstanding qualities? Are they gifted, good-looking, rich or otherwise endowed? Sure, some of them are bound to be, but most will be no more gifted, better looking, wealthier or more generously endowed than you or me because good fortune does not guarantee success in love.

The real difference between the haves and have-nots in love is that the haves command a firm grasp of the vital ingredients essential to make love grow and they know the recipe, perhaps intuitively, for making relationships work.

Until the publication of *Countdown to Love*, what was missing from today's culture of instant gratification was a genuine blueprint to the building blocks for establishing loving relationships that each and every one of us – no matter how dissimilar – can embrace. Now this blueprint is available to everyone who wants to meet Mr or Ms Absolutely Right and forge a loving and lasting relationship. There are no easy fixes or false promises in this book. To achieve magnificent twosomeness, readers must participate in the exercises.

Don't allow yourself to be put off if your love life has been disastrous or non-existent to date. Even if you swore you would never love again, read on. *Countdown to Love* is not simply a book that will capture your imagination and enable you to test whether or not your new or existing partner is the one for you. It is also a philosophy of love that works for men and women of all ages, and it can deliver your consummate partner sooner than you expect. Remember that Cupid helps those who help themselves.

The inspiration for *Countdown to Love* – the book and the seminar series conducted by David Matchmaker Hinds and his wife, Tatiana – is belief in the idea that life's greatest gift is love and life's finest pleasure is sharing it with someone special. If you agree with the premise but lack the special someone with whom to realise your dreams, then the Countdown phenomenon will interact with you if you let it, to steer you towards your ideal partner.

Perhaps you are already in love, happily married, or in a new or promising relationship? *Countdown to Love* will empower you to bring out the best in yourself and your partner and to create the foundations for a lifelong partnership.

Maybe you know, but would rather not admit, that you are trapped in a loveless, one-sided or abusive relationship that's going nowhere? *Countdown to Love* can help you to find the courage and the motivation to break free and provide you with the expertise to make the correct choice of partner when the time is right.

If you have given up on love and sentenced yourself to a life alone, *Countdown to Love* has the potential to rejuvenate your passion for romance, re-igniting your faith in humanity and injecting new meaning, depth and satisfaction into your existence.

Whatever your personal circumstances, *Countdown to Love* will provide six essential, state-of-the-art tools without which no one should contemplate their love life:

1 **An all-inclusive package** for getting yourself ready for Mr or Ms Absolutely Right.

2 **Realistic and do-able proposals** for meeting your ideal partner.

3 **A 20-point process** for enriching your love life and achieving magnificent twosomeness.

4 **The Matchmaking Equation** to enable you to find out NOW if your new or existing partner is *the one*.

5 **The recipe for lasting love** – a structured and step-by-step approach to winning in love.

6 **The Countdown,** which, in personal terms, is not unlike the checks that astronauts engage in before the launch of a space rocket. It is designed to ensure readers are equipped and ready to launch themselves into a meaningful relationship with the right partner. If this sounds melodramatic, take on board that a lasting relationship, like a trip to the Moon, is a phenomenon that so many people have yet to experience.

The aim of the book is a simple one: to help people meet their ideal partner and to enjoy the happiness of a lifelong relationship. *Countdown to Love* reveals everything men and women need to know about compatibility and the crucial differences between the sexes in communication styles, emotional needs and modes of behaviour. In this easy-to-understand operating manual you will find out if you have any aspects of your character that could wreck your love life and how best to negate them. Using the most powerful and life-changing tools and principles that are at the heart of all meaningful relationships, you will prepare yourself for love that will last.

Where should you start? At the juicy bits that leap from the page? At the chapter headings that have special significance to you?

At the unique and telling contributions written specifically for *Countdown to Love* by famous couples who share with you the essence of their long-running and highly successful marriages? You probably won't be able to stop yourself. But be aware that the Countdown format follows a relationship in logical sequence, commencing with the all-important pre-relationship primer, so the beginning is the place to start.

Part 1: Minus One provides you with a firm basis from which to understand the meaning of love and happiness. It allows you the freedom to assume the appropriate mindset to take advantage of the options that will be opening for you as you adapt to accommodate the ebb and flow of love.

Part 2: The Power of Attraction may sound like turning the lights down low and putting on mood music, but in fact, as well as dealing with flirting and the traps to avoid, it centres upon the uniqueness of you and the various ways you can enhance your individuality.

Part 3: Before Lighting the Touch Paper addresses sensitive matters like the ex, releasing the venom and freedom to start again. Any potentially hazardous matters (your best friends, the ghosts of lovers past, your occasional bouts of depression and the kids) are best dealt with here, not behind your back, or over a romantic dinner that terminates with the starters.

Part 4: Contact is where things could get scary, actually meeting people with real potential – if you were not so relaxed and well prepared, and you will be when you accept the Countdown philosophy. In fact, this is going to be pleasurable, easier to set up than you might suppose and rather fun.

Part 5: Romance deals with that loving feeling, celebrating what you have in common, recognising differences honestly –

even enjoying those differences – and probing to establish whether there is a basis for genuine commitment.

Part 6: The Matchmaking Equation helps you to navigate calmly and rationally through the intoxication of love. Don't take fright; it's not mathematics as you remember it, simply a strategy for finding out if your new or existing partner is the one for you in the long term. Are you up for this? You bet!

Part 7: Countdown to Love is the climax you have been working towards. Right here is where you discover the true value of your relationship and whether it has the capacity to last. This is the nearest you will ever get to fast-forwarding yourselves into the future and taking a mathematical peek at what life together could be like in 10, 20, 30 years from now. Are you and your partner destined for magnificent twosomeness or will you be history?

PART 1

Minus One

*On stage I make love to 25,000 people;
then I go home alone.*

Janis Joplin 1943–70

Can I get lucky?

We will either find a way or make one.

Hannibal 247–182 BCE

Imagine, for a moment, one of those huge Russian trawlers with its fishing net the size of a dozen juggernauts, dragging the ocean bed, scooping up fish by the lorry-load, not for consumption but in search of one particular species of fish and just one very special fish from that species. Our desire for the optimum partner and our need to be loved, happy and fulfilled is like that fishing net. In our own different ways, we are all searching for satisfaction in a less-than-perfect world and in this age of instant gratification we tend to cast an ever-widening net in the hope of getting what we want.

But many of us have yet to learn how to fish, or even how to choose promising waters. Or how to recognise a great catch if it stared us in the face and said, 'Hello, gorgeous, I want to spend the rest of my life making you happy. I will prove my love for you every day, without fail, until the day I die by making you feel more loved, more wanted, more excited and more treasured than anyone in the history of the world.'

The proverbial wisdom is, 'Give someone a fish and that person eats for one day. Teach them to fish and they eat for life.' This book aims to help you to develop the expertise to recognise and land the ideal partner and the skill to make a success of any viable relationship – even an existing one that appears to be heading south – together with the insight to eliminate those undesirable personal traits that have prevented you from becoming a permanent partner in a magnificent twosome up to now.

The act of purchasing this book demonstrates willingness on your part to move ahead to a new, more satisfying chapter in your life. You may have much to learn, of course, but everything of importance that you need to know about relationships is between these covers. It is my objective to make the learning curve illuminating and, where appropriate, fun. This book is about you, about your needs and about your ultimate success in achieving a lifelong relationship with the right person. Read on and you will feel yourself gaining in confidence, personal ability and charisma until you know you are ready to win in love.

We feel unlucky in love when we keep making bad choices in our relationships, or when we have no relationship at all. Guilt is a classic killer of luck, along with the inability to get over a regrettable event from the past. Sometimes we are so busy looking at the closed door behind us that we cannot see the one that is opening in front of us! I believe we all make our own luck to some extent. We get lucky in love when we are feeling relaxed and open to persuasion, when we have confidence in ourselves and we know, with absolute certainty, that we are worthy of winning the heart of the person who deserves us.

Lucky people meet their perfect partners, find fulfilling careers and achieve their lifelong ambitions so that they live happy and meaningful lives. Their success is not always due to them working especially hard or being exceptionally talented, gifted or clever – as a quick flick through the TV channels will confirm. Instead, they appear to have an uncanny ability to be in the right place at the right time and enjoy more than their fair share of lucky breaks.

Luck undoubtedly exerts a dramatic influence over our lives. A stroke of bad luck can ruin the best-laid plans, whilst a moment of good luck can guide you to the hand of your future partner. Luck has the power to transform the improbable into the possible, to make the difference between success and failure, hope and despair, life and death. But people who get what they want are not necessarily born lucky; they simply create good fortune, perhaps intuitively, by doing the things and adopting the attitudes that lead to favourable outcomes.

So-called lucky people are, in effect, conducting their lives in such a way that interesting people are attracted to them, bringing with them all sorts of exciting possibilities that might otherwise have passed them by. Being in the right place at the right time is more about being in a receptive frame of mind to take advantage of what life has to offer at any given moment than physically shifting your body to a timetable.

Think for a moment about a person you know whom you admire and would like to emulate. Regardless of whether they are married or not, do they have an enviable lifestyle, an assured independence, the apparent freedom to do as they wish and the charisma to draw others to them? If they have some of these things, is it luck, or is it the choices they have made that give the impression that good fortune is always with them?

Like the person you most admire, I believe you will go ahead and commit now to making the inspired choice to be wanted, sought after and desirable to be around so that others beat a path to your door. Why? Because this is the most effective way, and by far the most dignified way, to turn your love life around.

Let's get started. I would like you to maximise your chances of getting a partner to kill for, or to breathe new life into an existing relationship if that is your aim, by taking one small step in the direction of making your dreams come true before the end of this chapter.

Just try this two-minute experiment. Focus again on the person you most admire. If no one immediately springs to mind, you can still benefit enormously from this exercise by basing your thoughts on a film or TV character, celebrity or famous person who fits the mindset that follows. Are they receptive to new challenges? Do they act on their hunches and gut feelings? Are they optimistic and outgoing in their approach to life? How do they react when things go pear-shaped? Do they simply move on and get on with the business of living, rather than dwelling on misfortune or their mistakes if things go wrong? Do they have the knack of somehow snatching victory from the jaws of defeat?

Now concentrate on just one aspect – big or small, you choose – of their winning perspective on life and consider whether you can emulate it. Assimilate this feature, adopt it and make it work for you for real. This can be fun and easy to do and so rewarding for your future prospects in love. The next time you encounter a problem, disappointments or an opportunity, practise responding with a new approach. *What would have been their response?* By doing so, you give yourself the opportunity, the choice, to effect a subtle but important shift in your attitude to change, and we can develop that to give you added value, charisma and the means to get lucky in love.

 ## *The Bottom Line*

> To get lucky in love, you must first learn to adopt a winning mentality. Anyone can do it!

Relationships that work

*Having enjoyed being married to Leo for 42 years,
I can say that the secret of our marriage is bedsprings
creaking, not so much from sex but from laughter at
a million private jokes that hold us together.*

Jilly Cooper

One of the happiest things about writing this book has been the generous response to my request for support from people whose relationships are an example to the rest of us. In the run-up to Christmas 2003, I wrote to a number of people whom I admire whose relationship with their partner has spanned many years. They were invited to write a brief passage encapsulating the essence of their marriage for publication in *Countdown to Love* so that they could share the secret of their success with you.

By Christmas Eve, I had received positive responses from a wide range of magnificent twosomes, each of whom has a tremendous amount to offer to readers seeking a lasting relationship with the right partner. Their personal contributions are absolute gems: from a top novelist, two much-admired musicians, a former

Archbishop of Canterbury, a European Commissioner and a Member of the European Parliament; and from a married couple whose careers have covered a spectrum from high-level politics to rebuilding their professional lives in the spotlight of media glare. The New Year brought me a hand-written message from arguably the most famous married couple in British television. I am most grateful to all these people for giving me their original thoughts.

> '... Having enjoyed being married to Leo for 42 years, I can say that the secret of our marriage is bedsprings creaking, not so much from sex but from laughter at a million private jokes that hold us together ...'

Classic Jilly Cooper! Doesn't that epitomise the type of marriage most of us would like to be in? You can feel the love, the care and the sheer hilarity of it all.

Of course, there is no point in expecting to arrive at a fully developed relationship before you have even found a partner. The potential rewards, however, of identifying the building blocks in a partnership at this early stage in the book are almost immeasurable. We could all speculate about what are the building blocks, but we shall find out for sure what has been significant to our distinguished contributors and we will be able to add others that are important to our individual personality.

Glenys Kinnock, British MEP and wife of former British Leader of the Opposition and European Commissioner Neil, says:

> '... Neil and I have had a chat and you can quote us as saying: The essence of our relationship over 40-odd years since we met has been deep friendship and trust. There's nothing stronger in good times, or when things – particularly professional life – are rather challenging.'

This must be right. It's easy to appreciate how strong a relationship must be in terms of trust to sustain a partnership in a marriage of politicians where frequent and long absences are part of the pattern. Only people who have a deep understanding of what is required in the face of such difficulties can maintain a successful marriage. You only have to see a clip of film showing Glenys and Neil together to realise that they have achieved lifelong happiness.

Christine Hamilton – professional raconteur and wife of former British MP – cites four Ls:

'lust, love, laughter and luck'

as the components of a happy marriage. Picture, for a moment, Neil and Christine Hamilton's eyes meeting at the office for the first time and thoughts of 'I do fancy...' You can imagine the fun that such positive personalities generated and how it would develop into love. You can hear the laughter, at least until Neil's career began to come under threat.

Only people confident of their commitment could have kept on laughing during what followed. The luck they had in finding each other must have seemed to desert them and it is a tribute to their love and support of each other that they went out and re-established themselves in the media glare. Not all of it could have been to their taste, but they decided to go for it and their marriage has survived magnificently.

We all have our moments of good and bad luck. How we respond can affect our future happiness and wellbeing. Luck almost certainly plays its part when seeking to meet the right person. But luck – both good and bad – is more controllable than you might imagine.

The Right Reverend and Right Honourable Lord Carey of Clifton, former Archbishop of Canterbury (1991–2002), offers deeply helpful reflections on love and marriage.

'There is no such thing as the perfect partner or the perfect relationship – true affection and love merges from a constant

relationship based on tolerance and understanding. It is essential for a couple to have a great deal in common and a fierce commitment to stay together even when things get tough. If your wife or husband is not your best friend, a relationship is not likely to survive. As practising Christians my wife and I go along with the adage "those who pray together stay together".

We do not have to share the Archbishop's religious convictions to appreciate these observations and benefit from these values.

So far, a number of building blocks have emerged: lust (which for many of us is where it all starts), laughter, friendship, love, trust, tolerance, commitment, understanding and having a great deal in common. We shall deal with all of these, but at this stage, I would like to comment on 'a great deal in common'.

Many people would argue that opposites attract. It is certainly true that they can, but it is significant that our contributors who have sustained long and successful marriages clearly do have a great deal in common. John Dankworth and Cleo Laine, the internationally renowned jazz musicians, share a passion for music that binds them together.

'Our relationship has been blessed by music – a bonding factor for human kind the world over.'

When you see them performing on stage or in their roles nurturing young musicians, you can feel the quality of their partnership.

Richard Madeley and Judy Finnigan have demonstrated live on British television every weekday how much they have in common by carrying out so much of their professional lives in public. Having been a guest on their show for the launch of my first book, *After Stroke,* and seen for myself the almost magical way in which they relate to one another off camera as well as on, allow me to share some very intimate words of theirs with you.

Richard: 'I have no idea where Judy and I will be in three, even two years from now: all our futures lie below the horizon. But as long as, wherever it is, we're together, we'll be okay.'

Judy: 'As long as I have my family, my health and Richard, I count myself a lucky woman.'

We have been, without doubt, in the company of magnificent twosomes par excellence throughout this chapter. They encapsulate the building blocks for a lasting relationship and their respect for each other is clear and unambiguous throughout.

Some people – because of their genes, their inspired and stable upbringing, their personal qualities or perhaps their canny instinct or sheer good fortune – take naturally to the building blocks from which lasting relationships develop. Others – like me for much of my early adult life and, I suspect, many of my readers – need guidance to find happiness and completeness in love.

Countdown to Love is designed to take you, step by step, to the core of your ability to create and enhance a loving relationship with the right person. You will quickly learn to zoom in and focus on what it is that you need from your partner-to-be. Perhaps, for the first time in your life, you will begin to understand what shapes your destiny and your decisions in personal relationships. Only then will you be in a position to know for sure what motivates you in love, or instils you with fear at the prospect of commitment.

By the end of this book, you will have the opportunity to set yourself up for success in love by doing the Countdown. By then, you should be intellectually and emotionally equipped and ready to tap into your desire to get what you want: a magnificent twosome of your own.

 ### *The Bottom Line*

> Magnificent twosomes have much in common and a steadfast determination to stay together.

Love!
Can I have some?

*If you think you can do a thing or think
you can't do a thing, you're right.*

Henry Ford 1863–1947

The answer to my question is 'Yes' when you understand what love is and how to make the transition from falling in love to staying in love. Life's greatest gift is love, life's finest pleasure is sharing it with someone special, and that includes the high spots, the unmitigated disasters and those roller-coasting bits in between. You deserve life's greatest gift, regardless of whether you have made mistakes in love in the past or missed opportunities that might have been there for you.

Many people with misgivings about love have encountered difficulties in making the transition from falling in love to staying in love, or they have been in a relationship with a partner with this problem. Although love 'just happens' – often at the most inconvenient moment – it is imperative to understand what love is and to prepare for it. When you have finished *Countdown to Love,* you will be ready to experience lasting love.

But first, the question I am asked repeatedly at social gatherings and in my professional capacity: 'How come it always goes wrong for me?' Why do so many genuine and well-meaning people fall in love only to find later that love has deserted them? Why doesn't the ecstasy and the intoxication of love live on endlessly as in romantic fiction? Why can't I live happily ever after?

Of the many misconceptions about love, by far the most ill fated is the belief that falling in love is somehow the forerunner to staying in love. It is a delusion because the two are totally different experiences: one is spontaneous, all consuming and (consciously or unconsciously) sexually motivated and short-lived; the other is the voluntary determination of two people to love and respect each other for their mutual benefit. For one experience to merge seamlessly with the other, as so many people tend to take for granted, we need a clear understanding of what is going on.

Most ex-lovers fail to distinguish between the two distinct phases of a love affair because the falling in love bit has a momentum and magic all its own. The staying in love part requires adjustment, flexibility and tolerance. If none is forthcoming, misery and pain will result. One of the primary reasons why so many marriages and otherwise promising relationships end prematurely is because no bridge has been built between the two stages of love. Unless strong links to a lasting relationship are forged on several different levels before the falling in love stage ends, love will disappear. Love between two people can last a lifetime only when it is anchored to a committed relationship.

We could fall in love with someone whom we perceive to be the perfect partner; this individual could prove to be the most wonderful person in the world and still the initial impact will fade and the honeymoon end because falling in love is a temporary phenomenon. It is spellbinding while it lasts, starting usually with an extraordinary eruption of emotion, passion and excitement that is unsustainable at this intensity because it is but the prelude to what could eventually become a deep and lifelong romance.

The casualty rate between these two stages is shocking. Many couples never make it to this higher, richer, more satisfying level of love because the realities of modern life get in the way. Unlike the falling in love stage, the allure of togetherness for lovers that transcend this stage is not simply glimpsed, touched and lost; it becomes rejuvenating as they hold each other in their thrall. A different kind of love takes over; one that is infinitely more gentle and enduring compared to the wildness and drama of falling in love.

The sensation of falling in love is essentially an erotic experience. We do not fall in love with our children although we love them very much. We do not fall in love intimately with our friends of the same sex (unless we are gay) no matter how much they mean to us. We fall in love only when there is an underlying sexual motivation.

What happens when two people move beyond the falling in love stage is a gradual but progressive stretching and merging of the couple's ego boundaries and tolerance levels as they extend themselves as individuals and as long-term lovers. Together, they reach towards the greatest reward that life on Earth has to offer: a happy and fulfilling relationship that withstands everything life throws at it.

Not all of us get it right first time. But, some of us do. My Scandinavian daughter Johanna put me to shame when she was just 18. Intuitively, and without any encouragement from her absent dad, she attracted the right partner for her while still at university, a handsome young Swede named Andreas. Now, 10 years on, their relationship is stronger and sweeter than ever. They complement each other and it is important to each of them that the other feels supremely wanted and secure. In my judgement, they have already achieved the ultimate accolade of magnificent twosome. I only wish that I had had the sensitivity to treat her mother better.

Whether we believe it or not, we all have the potential to attract the partner who is right for us, and providing that we are willing to learn how to give and receive unconditional love and to make the progression from falling in love to a committed relationship, it will happen for us. If we want it enough, the precious, life-enriching experience of a love affair that lasts is within our reach, regardless of age, no matter where we live.

The Bottom Line

> Bridge the gulf between falling in love and staying in love.

Where do I start?

Do what you can, with what you have, with where you are now.

Theodore Roosevelt 1858–1919

Lasting love, unlike falling in love, does not just happen. It has to be cultivated. Already, in Chapter 2, you have taken a preliminary look at some outstanding relationships that have not only withstood the test of time, but also become sweeter and stronger through the trials of life over which they have triumphed.

As we progress through the book, we will isolate and examine the building blocks to lasting love that feature prominently in these winning relationships where both parties are happy. Here, we are simply going to acquaint ourselves with the basic ingredients from which relationships are formed. Love, in order to express itself within the context of a viable relationship, must consist, like the corners of a square, of four parts:

1 Lust (often referred to as 'passion' or 'physical attraction' because of the lecherous and sinful connotation of the word)
2 Friendship
3 Trust
4 Respect

A truly loving relationship between two people cannot exist for any length of time if one or more of these fundamental requirements is missing. I make no apology for stating the obvious because so many men and women who genuinely want a lifelong partner and do not have one have yet to acknowledge and embrace this incontrovertible fact of love.

The spark that can transform a chance encounter to loving status, or breathe new life into a stale marriage, must generate feelings of lust, friendship, trust and respect for the other person, and those feelings must be reciprocated. This is paramount for the establishment of a healthy relationship that will one day have the capacity to evolve into a multifaceted and lifelong romance.

If friendship and trust develop between two people along with mutual respect, but there is no lust for each other, the spark that sets off feelings of affection fails to ignite and there is no drive or momentum towards a loving relationship, denying romance the opportunity to take root. When lust alone is the raw driving force in a liaison, sex or a shallow affair is the best that can be hoped for.

Sadly, in my experience, many people – particularly if they are uncomfortable with their own domestic situation, lacking in self-esteem or lonely – settle, in desperation, for a relationship that cannot possibly last. These unfortunate individuals enter into inappropriate relationships, sometimes knowing that they are selling themselves short, because it satisfies their immediate superficial needs, or because they are unhappy to be on their own.

'Why does love always desert me?' they complain when the inevitable break-up occurs or the heartache sets in. You can imagine how popular I am when I point out that they did not have what constitutes a proper relationship in the first place. All they had was a mirage in the form of temporary comfort because the supposed relationship lacked one or more of the essential cornerstones to romantic fulfilment: lust, friendship, trust and respect.

Lust! What is it?

Whatever it is, it is something that you can't quite put your finger on. Why not? Because the word lust can mean different things to different people at different times. Generally, it is taken to mean a strong desire for sexual gratification, but this can be contradictory because it is possible to have an insatiable lust for someone without necessarily wanting to make love.

Lust is a significant factor in any robust and healthy relationship, but it is important to keep it in proportion. A couple who have fallen head over heels in love with each other probably feel, in the run-up to making love for the first time, 100 per cent lust for each other – nothing less! Although this red-hot level of lust is exhilarating in the short-term, it can't last at this intensity, even in the most passionate of relationships. While lust will continue to remain an essential component of love, friendship, trust and respect become increasingly important as a relationship matures.

Friendship

Before you can truly win someone's heart, you must first make a real friend of that person. Although this might appear straightforward, many people have trouble when it comes to demonstrating true friendship towards their lover. Genuine friendship involves meeting a person's deep emotional needs. So, what are these needs and how best can you meet them in the eyes of the person you want?

1 **Attention.** Show that person you are consciously aware of his or her existence.

2 **Appreciation.** Make it clear that you care about them and openly acknowledge any praiseworthy quality the other person possesses.

3 **Understanding.** Demonstrate your sincerity in striving to identify with how that person feels about things in general

and the world as a whole. Find out what is important to them.

4 **Compatibility.** Make every effort to expand and explore those interests that you share.

5 **Acceptance.** When it is necessary to show disapproval, use a non-critical demeanour to reinforce his or her value to you. Don't put up shields to protect yourself.

6 **Affection.** Regardless of how that person might compare with others, treat them like a VIP.

Trust

Trust, which is reliance on and confidence in the truth, comes easily to some people and is hard won by others. Looking back over my past relationships and marriages, I can see clearly now that, to my shame, I was not worthy of the trust invested in me by these wonderful women. If it suited me to cheat, I would, and if it was more convenient to fabricate than tell the truth, that is what I would do. The biggest single difference in my marriage to Tatiana and all previous relationships is the fact that I am worthy of her trust. We can rely on each other completely and this is such a wonderful thing in a relationship.

Respect

People are motivated to be with and associate themselves with people whom they really respect. Saying 'please' and 'thank you' are classic examples of respect, along with resisting the urge to interrupt or contradict your partner while talking, especially in front of others. Demonstrating respect for each other by responding considerately to their vulnerabilities and sensibilities is a sign of good character and an indication of the treatment you can expect and aspire to in the future. Your body language and eye contact will convey a similar message.

Giving your partner as much as, or preferably more than, he or she gives you – in all things – is a tangible statement of respect. If both partners adopt this philosophy, the result can only be happiness and contentment for both parties. Being treated with respect makes people feel happy, valued and special. The person who shows respect, commands respect.

And there you have it: the four cornerstones of lasting love, without any one of which a relationship is not a relationship that will survive.

 The Bottom Line

The quintessential elements of romance are lust, friendship, trust and respect. Build from there.

Let's do it

Nothing contributes so much to tranquillise the mind
as a steady purpose: a point on which the soul
may fix its intellectual eye.

Mary Shelley 1797–1851

In order to do anything with the certainty of success you must focus your mind on what it is you intend to achieve, the target of your ambitions must be so clearly implanted on your brain that the possibility of failure is removed. When that ambition is as personal and as worthy as winning the heart of the person who is going to love you until eternity, you can leave nothing to chance; you must use the most powerful tool for the purpose: the mission statement.

When I was younger, less enlightened and spectacularly unsuccessful in love, I would probably have turned my nose up at the mere suggestion that I should employ a device from a previous century. But it is to the mission statement that I can trace back the beginning of my good fortune in love. Until that moment when I sat down and committed my personal ambition to heart and to paper, I doubt if a single member of my family or any of my closest friends trusted in my ability to find lasting happiness in love.

'What makes you think I'm Superman?' I said to my wife, tongue in cheek, some years into our marriage, when she had addressed me as such. 'The fact that you managed to win me over,' she replied.

Master the power of the mission statement – in this chapter I shall show you how – and you give yourself the impetus to become a Superman or Superwoman to the person of your dreams. The act of preparing your own mission statement (providing you are genuine about every word you write) will ignite the urge within you to search with new vision, until you find that special person and win their heart and their admiration so that they fall in love exclusively with you.

Will you need to be beautiful, rich, fit or well to achieve this? Of course not! At the time when I wrote my mission statement, all I had was a plan to write a book, absolute sincerity, my friends and a banged-up Fiat Punto called Goldie that was destined to expire in the overtaking lane of the M4, en route to Heathrow airport.

After spending years recovering from serious illness, I decided to set myself the ultimate challenge: I resolved to find the perfect partner and marry her within 18 months. I had no doubt that I would succeed. What surprised my new wife and me was that we had met years before in London but never seen each other as potential lovers.

Although I had experienced disaster and misfortune, I had a vision of life free from the disability and solitude of long-term illness; a vision that included doing something useful with my life that would not unduly tax my stroke-ravaged body, like writing a book. I have always been an optimist, even with despair staring me in the face, so naturally that vision included living happily ever after with the perfect lover. If you want to turn your dream of domestic bliss into reality, make your vision the overriding picture and purpose of the life you're aiming towards. Committing your purpose to paper and placing it somewhere conspicuous so that you see it until it becomes reality is a tangible step towards making it happen.

The most critical variable for your success in finding Mr or Ms Absolutely Right is *you*. It is easy to assume that circumstances must be just right in order for you to meet your future partner, but in fact, even if the circumstances are favourable, you can only take advantage of them if you are focused on what you want to achieve. If you're not in the right frame of mind to realise your vision, if your purpose is not imprinted on your brain and embedded in your heart, you could be holding the perfect partner in your arms and never know it.

In order to be in the right frame of mind to realise your dream when opportunity strikes, it is helpful to build rapport with yourself. Building rapport with yourself requires careful attention and a genuine respect at a deep level for your personal mission in life: your need for love, happiness and fulfilment.

When the time comes to write your personal mission statement, as it will at the close of this chapter, the words you write must ring true and gel with your heart, your soul and your rational mind. If not – if you deceive yourself into thinking you want something to which you are not committed – your love life will end up empty or in turmoil, because a part of you wants this and another part of you wants something else. This is a very common experience with individuals who lack internal rapport and frequently results in the wrong choices being made by those who have yet to decide the direction of their life.

When we build rapport with someone else, we tend to start the process by acknowledging 'where that person is' from our interpretation of their perspective on life. This means accepting at face value the other person's position and what is important to them, and showing that acceptance both verbally and by means of our body language. It means recognising where they are in their thoughts and their experiences at the present time, rather than leaping in with judgements or opinions of our own.

The same applies when you set about establishing rapport with yourself. Start from where you are now, warts and all, not some imaginary scenario in which you would like to be, because total honesty with yourself is the essence of a mission statement that works. There is no need to pretend that everything is great simply because you are demonstrating your wisdom and willingness to change right now by finding out how to bring love into your life.

Rapport founders just as much on unrealistic praise as on unrestrained criticism of our little weaknesses and imperfections. We know we aren't perfect, but today we need to know we are at one – heart, soul and mind – when we key in or write the words of our personal mission statement on the love we want and deserve. Typically, this statement will be no longer than two paragraphs. The first, by way of a brief statement about yourself, including who you are, what you do and why you do it; the second, a simple affirmation of what it is that you want from your love life. Remember to include the date. When you look back with fondness at what you have achieved, I want you to take pride in how quickly you turned your love life around.

When we build rapport with ourselves, it becomes easier to focus unwaveringly on what we really want, because inner doubt is alleviated or vanquished. We create a situation both internally and externally whereby we can start to move forward in the direction of our dreams, without part of us wanting to hold back or quit.

Now is the ideal opportunity to boost rapport, because the degree of honesty and openness with yourself required to create a telling mission statement – one with which you can be completely at peace – will test you. People seldom get their true thoughts on the love they want and the love they are prepared to give right first time. It may take several attempts to get your thoughts lucid in your mind, but persevere until you have a crystal-clear statement of intent before you. You'll know when you do have it right. It will feel 'you' and you will feel good about yourself. The benefits of what you are about to do are threefold: you focus your awareness on the relationship you need; you build rapport with yourself by identifying what is missing from your life; and you make everything possible by committing your intentions to paper.

A mission statement is not a wish list. It is statement of intent to someone very important – *you* – that you intend to act and make things happen. It is more substantial than a decision. When you make a decision, one you mean to keep, you draw a line, not in the sand but in cement. You know exactly what you want. This kind of clarity gives you the power to do even more to get the results you decided to go for. When you commit yourself to a mission statement, you go further and deeper than the most decisive decision can take you; you cut off any other possibility than the one that you have decided to make your personal reality.

Don't set out to impress yourself or anyone else with elaborate wording. This really is your life you are going to forecast and the all-important ingredients of this statement are truth, realism and personal integrity. Regardless of whether you are in your 30s, 40s, 50s, 60s, 70s or 80s, the document you are about to prepare for your own exclusive use is of paramount importance to your future happiness. It is the future! So potentially rewarding is the next step that I am prepared to break the rule of a lifetime and show you my personal mission statement from many years ago, in the hope that it may inspire you to reach into your heart and prepare your own. You can ignore the first paragraph, as I was dealing with both my professional and personal life.

David M Hinds
Polperro, Cornwall
17th February 1999

I shall dedicate myself to writing as my profession. I am doing this with my life because I get tremendous satisfaction from the results of my writing. I regard the letters of appreciation from readers that are forwarded on to me by my publishers as a measure of my success. I am happy and enthused by this, my third and final career.

This year I will endeavour to find someone to love and cherish who is uniquely desirable, someone who will love me forever and be happy living here in Polperro. I will be truthful, kind and faithful to her and do everything I can to deserve her love. We will be friends as well as lovers and lifelong partners.

Forget about all past mistakes and disasters; get this right and you will live a dream come true. Write your statement now and start an adventure that will prove too good to miss.

 ## The Bottom Line

Do it now! Prepare your personal mission statement: transform your dreams into reality.

CHAPTER 6

PART
1

When do we meet?

It is a mistake to look too far ahead. Only one link of the chain of destiny can be handled at a time.

Winston Churchill 1874–1965

Ironic though it is, now that you are sharpening your interpersonal skills in preparation for the relationship of a lifetime, you will meet your love match when you learn to relax and accept the Countdown premise that you must let go of your anxiety for romance to happen.

I am not in favour of aggressive American man-hunting techniques typified by books like *The Program* by Rachel Greenwald. Personal relationships are much too complex and important to be straitjacketed into a strict formula. With *Countdown to Love,* you are not required to run around embarrassing yourself and your entire network of friends, pursuing potential partners until your legs cave in. Instead, you are encouraged to relax, to expand your social scene at your own pace and to expel worry from your dating so that the real you is visible.

Think again about the person you most admire, the exercise you engaged in towards the end of *Chapter 1: Can I get lucky?*

Do they have desperation in their eyes, exhaustion in their soul, a bankrupt social scene, or do they adopt a relaxed, interested, but laid-back approach to the good things in life? Let's get smart! Mr or Ms Absolutely Right will be attracted to you when you send out the right signals. When it is clear that you are in control of your destiny, you know what you want in life and you are prepared to hold out, enjoying life in the meantime, until you are moved to open your heart at the perfect moment. That is when you will meet your ideal match.

Nothing has to change in the real world to bring about this transformation in your prospects, other than a tiny shift in your perspective on life and willingness on your part to absorb the nuggets of information that will enable you to allow romance to enter your life. Have you ever noticed, when you need something desperately – a taxi, a phone call, love – it never comes, but when the emergency is over, the crisis has passed, you have given up waiting and moved on, along comes a convoy of taxis, the phone rings, love walks in?

Encouraging you to be relaxed about finding love might seem like contradictory advice as it is coming from the same person as the one who is preparing you for the relationship to end all relationships, but the anxiety about your single status has got to go, along with any obvious enthusiasm to get hitched. Nothing is more unattractive than desperation!

Okay, after finishing the last chapter, you spent hours perfecting your personal mission statement (which I want you to read and reread every day until it becomes obsolete, due to the constructive steps you take) and now I'm telling you to relax and let go? Not quite! That document is your passport to a future shared. Letting go does not mean giving up on love or adjusting to being single, or even that you are no longer actively looking for love. It simply means that you choose not to worry or get anxious about the need to find the right relationship. This is a pivotal distinction and one that you must get your head round in order to give yourself a head start in the love stakes.

Letting go of the downside of being single – the worry, the fear, the emptiness – brings a wonderful feeling of release. It makes a powerful statement to you and everyone you meet – including your future partner – that you like yourself, you are in harmony with what's going on in your life and you are nice to be with. Reinforce this message and you will come face to face with the person who is right for you sooner rather than later.

Letting go is the joy of parting with an unwanted burden, a sense of inner peace, of accepting life as it unfolds, which you can do with ease now that you are taking positive steps to ensure that you win in love. All that you are being encouraged to let go of is the ugly aspect of life as a singleton; the struggle, the panic and the longing for things to be other than they are. Letting go is a demonstration of your trust in the Countdown philosophy and belief that things will go according to plan (now that you have a plan), the starting point of which is your mission statement.

Actually letting go of anxiety is a two-part process over which you do not immediately have overall control. Part of letting go is recognising that you don't have all the answers now, but having confidence in the knowledge that as you progress through the book, you will be wiser and more receptive to new ways of doing things that will lead to success.

The other part of letting go is fascinating because you can't make it happen, you can't will it to happen, it just creeps up on you in its own good time and works its magic because you somehow managed to off-load your anxiety about your solo existence.

Most people are not even aware of the subtle changes that are taking place within them, because they are absorbed in the detail of the Countdown approach and the positive planning that entails. Somebody else will notice the change in you.

One day, a member of your family, a friend, or perhaps someone at work will say something like this, 'What's happened to you – you seem different?' You know, at this point, you are a step closer to meeting your match.

The Bottom Line

Relax; enjoy your single status. It won't last long if you adopt the Countdown philosophy.

PART 2

The Power of Attraction

Intensity of attraction is a beautiful thing. But to mislabel it love is both foolish and dangerous.

Stanton Peele

CHAPTER 1

PART
2

First impressions

A man falls in love through his eyes,
a woman through her ears.

Woodrow Wyatt 1919–97

We all possess the power of attraction – the ability to make a favourable impression on people and retain their interest. But how many of us know how to direct this power, using it, for instance, to reach out to the person we want, affecting them as if they were spellbound and hypnotised by our charm?

Make no mistake, the power of attraction is predominantly an internal thing, not simply the good looks that some are born with and others buy at the cosmetics counter, or receive from the sharp end of a surgeon's knife. Do we know what is going on when we first attract someone? Or when we feel attracted and drawn to a particular individual? What is the power we exert over them and they over us when we are making that all-important first impression?

In order to answer the questions we need to address two issues. Firstly, we need to know what it is that naturally excites people and attracts their attention, and secondly, we must become aware of our own authentic self. Be warned: one without the other will not deliver you to magnificent twosomeness. To be effective, you must incorporate your knowledge of what attracts people – we'll work on this – into your everyday life so that the uniqueness of you is intensified in the minds of other people.

If, like many people, you rely predominantly on your physical attractiveness to make a favourable first impression, you may acquire new friends and associates with ease, but a permanent and meaningful relationship will not necessarily result. Only developing and blending your natural powers of attraction with those personal traits and features of your identity that are unique, will deliver potentially the right partner for a loving relationship with the realistic expectation that it should last. Furthermore, you will become a more interesting and sought-after person, regardless of the colour of your skin, the shape of your face, your sexual orientation or your physique.

Most of us are attracted to those people that others find attractive. Few are drawn to the person others avoid or neglect because our desire for another person usually involves social considerations, as well as personal ones. To draw people closer to you and make them interested in you, you must create an aura of desirability. Our minds are constantly barraged with competing images, not just from advertising and the media, but also from the day-to-day trials of our very existence, and many of these images are so striking that you run the risk of being forgotten in an instant unless you leave a lasting impression. In the brief window of opportunity that a meeting or unexpected encounter affords, you must engage the imagination of that person, sparking the more haunting kind of spell that makes them think about you long after you have gone.

In the next chapter, you will have the opportunity to get to know yourself like never before, but it would be helpful now if you had some idea how others perceive you when they meet you. What is the first impression they form in their mind about you? In order to be able to answer this question, we need to be able to identify your key features: the well-defined, memorable and distinguishing features and characteristics about you that others immediately latch on to.

You probably already have some idea about this from the way that your friends and acquaintances relate to you. It's important to learn more about the snap decisions people make about you and what motivates these judgements, because they can help you to summarise and select which particular facets of yourself that you might want to highlight or tone down to make a better impression.

Your future partner may be someone that you meet by chance and he or she may only have a few moments in which to decide if they want to get to know you better. This is precisely how I met my future wife and perfect partner-to-be. We met on the pavement outside the British Museum in London when Tatiana stopped me to ask for directions. Neither of us had any inkling at that time that we would go on to become friends and lovers, but we certainly made a memorable impression on each other! This is why I feel so strongly that you must hone and perfect your first impression skills because, like mine, your time will come.

First impressions are always formed from a combination of physical and hidden characteristics – outer and inner qualities that gel (or not) and leave a favourable or unfavourable impression. We are all complex individuals: compilations of many different personality traits, moods and physical features, and our most distinctive features are not always obvious or easy to identify.

You may like to rope in a friend or two to help run through the 11-point plan that follows to tease your unique compilation out of you. Tatiana and I will be guinea pigs so that you can have a good laugh at our expense, before getting stuck in yourself.

To begin, all you have to do is note down a few pertinent words of description about yourself for each of the ten categories that follow. I am a great believer in simplicity, so when you have completed this assignment we shall refer to it in future as the ME document.

The ME document

Highlighting the distinctive features about
..........................(your name)

1 **First glance:** How others perceive you.
2 **An informed opinion:** How your family and friends see you.
3 **Type of person:** What sort of person you are.
4 **Social skills.**
5 **Your professional skills** (which include parenting, if applicable).
6 **Your love driver:** It can only be one of three – in relationships, your heart, your head or a healthy combination of both drives you.
7 **Prominent sense:** You use all five of your senses in order to see, touch, smell, taste and hear, but which one assumes pole position in your love life?
8 **Special qualities:** Those qualities that people who know you admire.
9 **Surprising aspect:** The part of you capable of astonishing even those who know you well.
10 **Hidden undertones of your personality:** Your dark, mysterious side.
11 **Your signature snapshot.** You are going to narrow your observations down to the three most potent words that sum you up in the eyes of other people. These three words we shall call your signature snapshot. After all, when we first set eyes on someone, most of us take just two or three seconds to decide if we like them or not, and whether we want to get to know them. To validate your signature snapshot, simply make sure that the description you select for Category 11 is derived from entries in Categories 1–10.

Here are two examples, first mine, then Tatiana's, of how to do it. Be as candid with your observations as possible. No doubt, your friends will need no such invitation! The object of the exercise is to sharpen your awareness of yourself and how other people see you.

The distinctive features about David Hinds

1 **First glance:** Relaxed but knows what he's about.
2 **An informed opinion:** Unpredictable – can be fun-loving and serious in turn.
3 **Type of person:** Heterosexual, creative, temperamental, perfectionist.
4 **Social skills:** Warm-hearted, inspirational, entertaining.
5 **Professional skills:** Award-winning stress counsellor, motivating writer.
6 **Love driver:** Heart.
7 **Prominent sense:** Touch.
8 **Special qualities:** Perseverance and can be relied on to deliver.
9 **Surprising aspect:** Can be confrontational.
10 **Hidden undertones:** Tendency to be outrageous.
11 **Signature snapshot:** Relaxed, inspirational, motivator.

The distinctive features about Tatiana Hinds

1 **First glance:** Slim, stylish, happy in herself.
2 **An informed opinion:** Serious – not to be trifled with.
3 **Type of person:** Heterosexual, intelligent, together, passionate.
4 **Social skills:** Highly accomplished swimmer, dancer and ice-skater.
5 **Professional skills:** Mathematician, co-author and teacher.
6 **Love driver:** Head and heart.
7 **Prominent sense:** Olfactory (smell).
8 **Special qualities:** Makes maths sexy and relevant, takes learners with her.
9 **Surprising aspect:** Adventurous – fell in love with an older man.
10 **Hidden undertones:** Will attack like a demon if slighted or unfairly criticised.
11 **Signature snapshot:** Centred, intelligent, loving.

Okay, you get the idea! Let's get going, but do make sure that the words you select accurately describe you. They must ring true to you and those who know you well. There is a hidden bonus for you in doing this; not only will you become more aware of your outstanding features so that you can use them (or play them down) to your advantage, but you will also have completed the groundwork for a more in-depth procedure that comes soon.

In the next chapter, we will look closely at the uniqueness of you. In the meantime, don't forget one of the major weapons in attracting people or being attracted to them – the smile. Smiling is by far the most pleasing and response-initiating aspect of body language that you can use to engage another person's attention. A smile instantly conveys confidence, a friendly disposition and a positive attitude, giving others the impression that you are in a good mood and fun to be with. It also makes a clear statement that you are approachable and open to persuasion, increasing your chances of getting to meet the person on the receiving end of that smile.

The Bottom Line

The power of attraction is deeper than skin-deep. It is something that radiates from within.

The uniqueness of you

It's not what I do but how I do it. It's not what I say but how I say it. And how I look when I'm saying and doing it.

Mae West 1892–1980

Armed with that winning smile and your signature snapshot from the previous chapter, we are going to seek to discover the uniqueness of you: the special mix of qualities and experiences that distinguishes you from everyone else. We will achieve this by expanding your signature snapshot into a fully developed portrait of you. The naked truth, in fact.

Each of us has a different personality – our individual pattern of emotion, behaviour and perception. If you say, 'I am not myself today' – everyone knows what you mean, but if you are not yourself, then who are you? Although you might think that you know what type of personality you have and your behaviour may indeed be consistent with it, occasionally you are bound to do something out of character. How do you explain that?

There are many theories as to what constitutes personality and how it develops. Some believe it is shaped through our experiences in life. Others believe it is genetic or developed in early childhood. Another view is that it is related to the environment, society or family. One thing is for sure: personality is not set in stone. People can change and they frequently do, perhaps as a result of altered circumstances, an inspirational book or seminar, or simply because they have made a conscious decision to improve or highlight one aspect of their character.

The primary way to achieve this is to become more self-aware. Getting to know someone else requires a certain level of interest and trust to be established. We develop this interest and trust by nurturing the relationship. Now that we are going to find out more about our own identity, we need to apply this same level of interest and trust to the internal relationship we have with ourselves that we tend to take for granted.

If, like many people, you treat yourself badly – by being overly self-critical and blaming yourself for situations that didn't work out – trust in your ability to get things right in the future will be undermined. Consequently, interest in the immediate prospect of enlightened self-exploration may be lukewarm and in need of stimulation.

Self-awareness calls for self-nurturing in order to be forward-looking, focused and ultimately beneficial to your ambition of establishing a lasting relationship with the right partner. How do we go about it? One method is to reflect on the way you would treat a small innocent child. If that child was hungry, you would feed it; if it cried, you would comfort it; if it made a mistake, you would forgive it; if it fell over, you would pick it up and help it back to its feet. You would encourage this child in every way you knew. When this child falls over you don't curse it. If the child drops a toy, you don't criticise it. The child is free to make mistakes because you know that is how it learns. The child develops through love and support.

Do you treat yourself in this caring way? Do you love and nurture yourself? Do you lift yourself up with fondness and care every time life knocks you down, comforting yourself when you are sad? Do you forgive yourself when you make a mistake, or do you punish yourself with harsh words of recrimination?

Hopefully, you are supportive of yourself, secure in the knowledge that you are a unique and wonderful person, worthy of love. Or close to that! If this is you, then you already know that you are too good to hold back or put down. Unfortunately, most of us have yet to learn not only to love and to nurture ourselves but also to stop abusing ourselves! We need to quit humiliating and undermining ourselves, because every time we do this we eat away and eventually destroy our sense of self-worth: the perception we hold in our minds of our unique identity; our personality as others and we know it.

To whom do you talk most? Your best friend, perhaps, a member of your family, your colleagues at work? No! The person you talk to most is yourself! Virtually everyone has an amazing internal dialogue with himself or herself. Are we kind and supportive in what we say to ourselves? Not a bit of it! Many of us are harsher and crueller in our choice of words and the rasping manner in which we deliver them to ourselves than any jailer would be.

Before we can safely peel away the layers of your identity to reveal the uniqueness of you, we really should put a stop to the bad-mouthing many of us subject ourselves to. What was it that you said to yourself the last time you reversed your car into a supermarket trolley? Or appeared a fool in front of someone that you rather liked?

The reason you really must put an end to self-inflicted, debilitating and demoralising assaults upon your ego is twofold. I need you to be totally honest in your dealings with yourself in preparation for a special assignment I have in mind for you later.

Continue to allow an acrimonious voice to ambush you at every turn – your very own live-in critic – and you will find it difficult to graduate with flying colours from this stature-enhancing exercise to come.

Also, with the safety net of the Countdown ahead of you, you will be taking more risks in future. You might get things right first time, but you might not. I don't want you to suffer the indignity of hearing an unkind or accusing voice berating you for having the guts to get out there and try for magnificent twosomeness; and make no mistake: to have a partner who means everything to you, and to whom you are the most wonderful person in the world, is not only worth striving for, but it is also the greatest achievement to which two people can aspire.

Some of the most common factors that prevent people from looking at themselves with enquiring eyes are the internal obstacles we construct for ourselves. If you really want yourself and others to experience the uniqueness of you, now is the time to make a decisive choice! Will you keep that internal voice of yours under control and train it to be your greatest supporter, or will you continue to allow it to be a critic and a killjoy, putting every conceivable barrier in your way and jeopardising your efforts to find the right partner for you? No one lives happily ever after in love unless they have first made peace with themselves and this is why this chapter is destined to be a tough one for many single readers.

Make a point of catching yourself red-handed the next time you bad-mouth yourself. When you do, say 'Stop!' in a friendly but authoritative tone of voice. Now get pen and paper and list everything derogatory that the voice has had to say. Look long and hard at that list. This is you we are talking about, the lovely, well-meaning you! Replace each harsh word on your list with something positive, gently reminding your internal voice that you are on the same side, that support and encouragement is what you need and what you expect in the future. If you are anything like me, you might have to run through this routine a few times before things start to move in the right direction.

Many people who live their lives without the support of a loving partner – someone who will love and admire them through thick and thin – are terrified of embarrassing themselves. The thing to remember about embarrassment is that it is a hundred times more awful for you than anyone else. The reality is that colleagues, workmates and general acquaintances don't care about your discomfort; they have their own lives to live. Sure, you might be the talk of the town for a day or two, but someone else is out there right now doing something perfectly ghastly that will be the topic of discussion for tomorrow and the next day.

If you allow your life to be governed by the need never to be humiliated, wrong or embarrassed, you will miss much of what life has to offer, and the chances are you will forfeit the opportunity to meet your match. Lighten up! Foul-ups and assorted calamities are part of the rich tapestry of life. Physical imperfections or blemishes upon your image are only a problem when you torture yourself with them. Others might find them attractive or amusing or might not notice them at all and you can always seek to improve things, should you need to. You will have just such an opportunity at the end of the chapter when you complete a programme of self-exploration. Yes, very soon now, we are going to discover the uniqueness of you, in all your complexity!

By the time we reach 30, most of us protect ourselves from the harshness of life by succumbing to routines and patterns, by hiding in the shadows of conformity. But underlying these habits is a tremendous sense of insecurity and defensiveness that can only be dispensed with by finding out what it is that makes you special, and by incorporating these unique features into our everyday persona, rather than smothering them. The real tragedy with so many of us is not that we don't have uniquely desirable features, it's that we fail to recognise what they are and use them to our advantage.

Our ideas and beliefs are largely culture bound and family determined because as children we learn from those around us. If we feel limited in some way, we need to look at our belief structure and challenge where these ideas originated. Are we trying to be someone that we are not, are we living by somebody else's ideals? Only you know where you have come from and where you want to be. Only you know what it is like to be you. Only you can successfully complete the exercise at the end of this chapter to find your unique identity. Unlike the previous exercise to reveal your signature snapshot when it was okay for your friends to lend a hand, don't allow anybody to help you this time, no matter how well-meaning their intentions.

What you are about to achieve by exploring your identity will enable you to appreciate and feel proud of your uniqueness as a very special individual. By taking the trouble to get to know yourself better, you will be more willing and ready to recognise and respect the differences in other people. The very act of probing yourself to find out what it is that's missing from your life makes it easier to find. This leap forward in personal development will empower you to boost your self-image, setting yourself up for more meaningful and lasting relationships in the future.

Don't worry if, in the course of self-discovery, you realise that you could do with sharpening your self-image, building greater self-esteem or increasing your confidence. Conveniently, these topics are next on the agenda.

Before starting this two-part exercise, have your personal mission statement and your ME document (which incorporates your signature snapshot) to hand. They will help to put you in the right frame of mind and keep you focused on the need to know yourself before you can live in harmony on a permanent basis with someone else.

Part 1: Your personal assets

When you are ready, consider the pleasing aspects in relation to each of the distinctive features that appear in your ME document. Expand the entries from a few words to a few lines, trusting yourself and only yourself to give an informed opinion for every category.

In many cases, the first thoughts that enter your head will be valid, or with further probing they might lead you to the compelling lines of portrayal that are very definitely you.

Part 2: The sharp questions

The questions for this assignment are aptly named because, of necessity, you will find them sharp, invasive and soul-searching as you rise to the challenge of addressing them truthfully and in full. The answers are within your grasp and when they come they are for your eyes only. What you are probing for is the uniqueness of you laid bare, without the trappings of uniformity behind which so many of us withdraw when it suits us!

Relax, get yourself comfortable and contemplate each question until you have the answer, the complete answer, in plain English – not psychobabble, clever terminology or legal jargon! You may find the questions that follow a little challenging: most people do. If the going gets tough, give yourself a break and come back to it in an hour or two. The pay-off comes later, not right now.

Okay? No time like the present for this, the final part of your self-realisation activity.

- Do you like yourself? If not, why not? What must change to improve your self-image?

- What is the most wonderful thing about you?

- Who has been instrumental in improving your life and to whom have you been helpful?

- Has a friend or partner ever betrayed you? If so, have you come to terms with this yet?

- What is it (non-materially) that is missing from your life?

- What do you want from your life partner and what are you willing to give in return?

- What is your sexual orientation? What are your carnal preferences? Be specific.

- What is the most satisfying aspect of your life now?

- What do you fear that you might lose if you commit fully to loving your partner (to-be)?

- What will it take to make you happy and fulfilled? Be explicit.

- Write down and relive in your mind your greatest achievement.

- Precisely what (other than reading this book) are you going to do in the next 10 days that could realistically be expected to begin to turn your love life around?

Well done! If you found this part of the programme easy, you are one of the lucky few. There is one final check to run and then your assignment will be complete and you can enjoy a well-earned rest. Look again at your answers to the sharp questions above. Are there any inconsistencies or contradictions between the response to one question and another? If you find any, you may wish to clarify which of the opposing responses is valid.

You should now have a clear and unequivocal picture of the real you, complete with a definition of your specific needs from a loving relationship. Furthermore, unless you already enjoy a healthy and informed relationship with yourself, within 48 hours of completion you should experience a wonderful feeling of relief, as if you have freed up an invisible block and empowered yourself. By then, you will be one step closer to realising your dream of magnificent twosomeness – and you will have every right to feel very proud of yourself.

The Bottom Line

Know yourself before expecting to live in harmony on a permanent basis with someone else.

Sharpening your self-image

What lies behind us and what lies before us are tiny matters, compared to what lies within us.

Ralph Waldo Emerson 1803–82

Your self-image defines and limits your possibilities as a human being. Unless you can genuinely imagine yourself winning the heart of the person you want and living happily together with them, it may never happen. In order to accomplish anything worthwhile in life, you must first believe that you can do it. The purpose of this chapter is to give you the opportunity to reassess your self-image, to challenge any limitations that you or other people may have placed on it and to sharpen your awareness of your true capability.

Virtually anyone of any age in the developed world, male or female, can win the person of their dreams and aspire to a happy, loving relationship, providing they believe in themselves and their self-image is comfortable with that aspiration. Should you doubt the integrity of that statement, then consider a very pertinent example for which I can affirm the accuracy of the facts.

How do you think I felt, staring at the ceiling from my hospital bed after my second stroke, knowing that I was partially paralysed and contorted, brain-damaged and unable to speak intelligibly or comprehend the written word, while my business disintegrated without me? I admit it took several years to recover both my health and my self-image, but even when the prospects looked grim I never gave up hope of finding the most wonderful woman in the world. Now this woman is my wife. Together, with your co-operation, we are going to help you move heaven and earth to make sure you get the kind of love and happiness we are enjoying.

Enough of the pep talk, let's do some real work sharpening your self-image so that you feel comfortable and positive about your very reasonable and natural desire for lasting love, and your chances of enjoying it sooner rather than not at all. The first thing to do is to give yourself the credit you deserve for your achievements. If these don't immediately flood to mind and make you blush with pride, think hard and you will find evidence galore with which to sharpen your self-image.

In the last few chapters alone you have done much to prepare yourself for magnificent twosomeness. That is an achievement that some people live their entire lives without even contemplating, let alone getting stuck in as you have done. Then there are all those things that you do particularly well. And the admirable and distinctive qualities that you have as a person, the positive aspects of you, quite apart from all the good things you have done in your life.

You need to recognise and acknowledge the finer aspects of you, because people are readily drawn to those who radiate a positive self-image, and I want you to be wanted. When you know, without a shadow of doubt, that you are worthy of the great love, you won't be able to stop yourself radiating a positive image and you will be very much in demand.

People pick up vibes from those around them. Think for a moment about those people that you enjoy being with the most.

They have a tendency to send out positive vibes and that's one of the reasons why you enjoy their company. Doesn't it make sense to radiate the same sort of vibes to other people? It's easy when you're relaxed and feeling good about yourself, when the image you have of yourself is sharp, focused and assured.

In order to sharpen a shaky or underdeveloped self-image, we will build on the self-awareness exercises from previous chapters that you have already completed. Write down all of the aspects of yourself that you actually like, including character traits, talents and achievements. Next, embellish this with the good things you have done for others and the reasons why you want and deserve the perfect partner.

Most people are surprised when completing this exercise by how much ammunition they possess to sharpen their self-image. If you don't experience this agreeable discovery, it could be that you are simply not in the mood, or perhaps you are feeling pessimistic. Try this simple exercise to get you back in touch with what you know to be true about yourself. It will help to re-establish your self-image and reassure you that you can win in the love stakes.

Write 'What I know to be true' at the top of a sheet of paper or at the start of a new file if you are using your computer. Create a list of the good things that you know to be true in your life. For example, depending on the truth of the statement, you might start with: 'I know that I'm friendly and honest.' Use the categories that follow as a point of departure to help you structure your list.

I know:

- I'm investing time and effort in reading a book about relationships

- A TV programme that makes me laugh

- Somebody who likes me

- Something I'm good at

- One personal quality I'm proud of

- Something I enjoy doing

- A way to make me happy

- One aspect about where I live that I like

- A kindness someone once showed me

- Something I did for someone else that makes me feel good

- There's always a chance I shall meet someone special and fall in love.

The final act of sharpening your self-image embraces the immensely powerful tool of the self-fulfilling prophecy. In the immortal words of Henry Ford who, as we all know, produced motor cars in an age when it wasn't the thing to do because there were no motorways to clog up: *'If you think you **can** do a thing or think you **can't** do a thing, you're right.'*

I say that you can find your ideal partner and enjoy the same degree of love and admiration for each other that Tatiana and I now share. If you think I'm right and you can do it, you're right, you can and will meet your match. If you think I'm wrong and you can't do it, you're right: you can't – and won't because your self-image defines and limits your possibilities as a human being.

The object of the next exercise is to expand your self-image so that you genuinely believe that you can get the lasting relationship that you want. It is always so much easier to achieve something when you're certain that you will succeed. If you don't believe you stand a chance, you don't! Take inspiration from my case. When I decided to write my first book, *After Stroke,* I couldn't read, let alone write.

If your expectations of success with *Countdown to Love* are low (perhaps you tried some other relationship book and it didn't work for you – there's so much dross out there) the 'empty chair' technique, which originally comes from Gestalt therapy, can help to expand the capacity of your self-image. Gestalt therapy is a version of psychotherapy that focuses on people recognising and changing the assumptions that hinder them.

This role-playing exercise that you conduct with yourself gives you the opportunity to express your expectations, to examine them and to come up with a more constructive outcome that in itself can be instrumental in making romance happen. Don't worry if you feel silly doing it for the first time. Most of us do! Do it anyway, because the benefits can be tremendous, far outweighing the minor discomfort of a few moments of apparent silliness.

The expectant self-fulfilling prophecy

- To get started, sit in a comfortable chair in a room on your own. Sit directly facing an empty chair. In your mind's eye, picture a virtual version of yourself sitting opposite you in the empty chair. Many people find it easier to close their eyes when engaging the 'speaking aloud' parts of this programme.

- Speaking aloud to your virtual self, in the chair opposite, state your reservations and negative expectations about your chances of finding the ideal partner. When you have expressed all your doubts, make a point of rounding off with a positive outcome.

- Now, swap places with yourself and argue to the best of your ability for your right to find the ideal partner – for example: When you first started school, you felt apprehensive but you made friends, all the same, didn't you? Well, why shouldn't you succeed again this time, but in a more significant way because you are older and wiser and you know exactly what you want from your relationship this time? Etc, etc...

- Swap places again so that you are sitting in your original chair. Repeat your positive arguments and expectations for success aloud again and feel your newfound trust and belief in your ability to succeed build up within you, as you become more optimistic. By changing your expectations, you are helping the all-powerful self-fulfilling prophecy to work in your favour. It is such a simple but potent tool with which to sharpen and polish your self-image.

- Now you have seen the shape of the exercise, you might like to repeat it in the next couple of days for a deeper experience.

You can confidently expect to project a sharper and more positive image in future. A positive self-image gives out reassuring vibes that are apparent in your facial expression, your speech and your general behaviour. These vibes are felt in the form of an aura that brightens the atmosphere around you, engulfing and captivating all those with whom you come into contact. People will enjoy being with you because of your personal magnetism, your charisma and the self-assurance that goes hand in hand with an enlightened self-image.

 The Bottom Line

> Your self-image defines and limits your possibilities as a human being.

Building
self-esteem

Not in the clamour of the crowded street,
Nor in the shouts and plaudits of the throng,
But in ourselves, are triumph and defeat.

H W Longfellow 1807–82

Look into a baby's eyes and see the joy and delight to be found there. You were once like this – enchanted by life, open and trusting, at the centre of your own universe. You felt free to express your emotions, you laughed and cried without hesitation, you willingly experienced everything that life had to offer.

We come into this world full of wonder. We accept ourselves, we accept the world and we accept everybody. We have no doubts and we have no preconceptions. We arrive with our sense of self-worth intact; we are full of self-esteem. It is only later that we learn self-doubt and how to be defensive so that we can protect ourselves from humiliation and harm. As we lose that coveted feeling of trust, so we lose self-esteem in equal measure.

It is easy to recognise when someone has high self-esteem. They are enjoying themselves to the full; they are able to be what they want to be and do what they want to do. They are, very definitely, their own human being.

Low self-esteem, once you have seen through the defensive layers of boasting, showing off, name-dropping, hogging the conversation and putting others down or sullen silence and withdrawal, is easy to spot. People who lack self-esteem no longer feel that they are in control of their experiences. They see themselves as victims, helplessly waiting to see what happens next instead of making things happen as they would like them to happen.

As you build self-esteem – and that is what you are going to do – you begin to feel good about yourself. You reclaim control over your life, becoming more flexible and resourceful, ready to respond at will to the ebb and flow of modern-day living. You start to enjoy the challenges that life presents and you are willing to tackle them head on. You feel powerful and creative and you quickly learn how to make things happen. As a direct consequence of building greater self-esteem, you become more open to persuasion, more willing to capitalise on a chance encounter, more likely to attract someone special into your life.

In my experience of negative emotions, which is what we feel when we are low in self-esteem, we don't necessarily get what we deserve. We get what we think we deserve. For many of us, the problem is that we don't think we deserve a lot when it comes to love and a meaningful relationship. As children we tend to believe what our parents tell us because we love and trust them and also because they are in authority. If we are told at a vulnerable age that we are not good enough, smart enough or likeable enough, we believe it! Furthermore, when we grow up, we may have difficulty in attracting or accepting the love we need. Likewise, the experience of loneliness, betrayal, divorce, or being dumped is bound to take its toll on our self-esteem.

Another cause of low self-esteem is guilt. Sometimes we feel too guilty to be loveable. If you done something you haven't forgiven yourself for or feel in some way responsible for someone else's pain, part of you may have concluded that you don't deserve to be loved. If you believe that you're unworthy of love, then any relationship you have will reflect this belief. If you feel that you don't deserve the best in life then, without doubt, you won't get the best. The quality of your life depends largely upon the quality of the relationship that you have with yourself.

Self-belief is the cornerstone of self-esteem. If I believe that I am worthless, no good and incapable, then my feelings about me will be reflected in my thoughts. My behavioural patterns will reflect my low self-opinion and so my whole experience of life, especially my love life, if I have one, will be low on quality and satisfaction.

When we are so lacking in self-esteem that we simply criticise and blame others or ourselves instead of doing something constructive to improve things, our behaviour will always be ineffective.

If, however, my thoughts about me are supporting and validating and I believe that I am intrinsically a worthy person who deserves self-respect, then my feelings about me will be correspondingly positive. Hence my behaviour will be creative and effective and I will succeed in making things happen in my life. Our self-belief, our thoughts about ourselves, directly affects our feelings that cause our behaviour. The good news is that we don't have to wait for things to change in the outside world. We can improve the quality of our lives by changing the way we think about ourselves. In so doing, we lay the foundations to bring our love life alive.

Self-esteem rests on self-acceptance, regardless of what we look like and what we are capable of doing. Liking comes after self-acceptance. Your liking for yourself will increase dramatically when you learn to accept yourself, the good bits and the shaky bits.

What are the main elements of self-esteem? People with high self-esteem have respect for themselves, they like themselves and they have a clear sense of purpose.

In order to facilitate further self-development it is important to differentiate between self-esteem and self-confidence. Self-esteem is more than just self-confidence. Self-esteem, quite literally, is the value we put on ourselves, whereas self-confidence relates primarily to action and the completion of tasks. I would be surprised if your self-esteem has not already been dramatically boosted by the exercises you did in the previous chapter. Nevertheless, there are further gains to be had.

Please ask yourself these questions
1   Can I take a compliment straight, without verbally deflecting it and without blocking and qualifying it in my head?
2   Am I afraid that one day someone will find out I'm not as good as people think?
3   Do I react positively to new and difficult challenges?

Did you manage to address and answer each question without hesitation, doubt or that sinking feeling? Many of us could benefit from building greater self-esteem, so let's take another look at those questions and see if we can ring some changes.

1   **Compliments!** The simplest and most effective way to take a compliment is by just saying, 'Thank you.' Allow yourself to hear and accept praise from other people; it is a healthy, legitimate and usually well-deserved boost to your ego.

2   **Being found out!** Ask yourself honestly: what is it I don't want other people to know? Probably, you don't want them to think as badly of yourself and your capabilities as you yourself do. Unless you are involved in some kind of fraud or dishonesty, this fear is usually unfounded and has more to

do with anxiety than reality. After all, most of us underestimate our capabilities at work and in our ability to win the heart of someone special, not overstate them. You only have to take an enquiring look at people who are contented to see that contentment and ability aren't necessarily connected. Equally, just glance at passing couples to be reminded that beauty is in the eye of the beholder.

3 **Reaction to challenge!** If you instinctively tell yourself you can't do something new because you might make a fool of yourself, you clearly have more work to do to make your internal dialogue more self-supportive. A positive way to make progress when you are next confronted with a challenge is to imagine that you are encouraging someone else to do well in this endeavour. Work out how you would help them. What words of encouragement would you use? Now use those words to motivate and reassure yourself.

How can you tell if someone has self-esteem? Is self-esteem observable from the outside? Sometimes, yes. One of the surest indicators is that people with good self-esteem don't feel the need to prove themselves. They don't:

- ✗ Put others down

- ✗ Boast

- ✗ Show off

- ✗ Name-drop

- ✗ Hog the conversation or display a tendency to be sullen or withdrawn

- ✗ Volunteer to tell you about their achievements.

People who behave like this often have quite low self-esteem, although allowances must be made for celebrities and those connected with the media and PR industries, who have a vested interest in blowing their own trumpet.

People with true self-esteem, even famous and highly successful people, usually exhibit very different patterns of behaviour. They:

- ✔ Have quiet confidence

- ✔ Don't fish for compliments – but they generally accept them: they know their value

- ✔ Recognise achievements in other people and are often interested in them

- ✔ Deal with external recognition without undue excitement or embarrassment

- ✔ Let their body language speak for them: they are often relaxed, upright, calm and decisive and they usually make good eye contact

- ✔ Might appear to have more than their fair share of good fortune.

As a direct result of the groundwork you have already done by completing the exercises in the previous chapters, you should now be in a position to build greater self-esteem with remarkable ease. Make a deliberate effort to avoid displaying the behaviours marked ✗ and try to adopt the behavioural patterns ticked ✔. Depending on your level of self-esteem now, in a few short days, and certainly in the weeks ahead, you should start to witness improvements in your self-esteem and the way that you feel about yourself.

 ## *The Bottom Line*

> When you are high in self-esteem you feel good about yourself and you draw others to you.

CHAPTER 5

PART
2

The confidence to succeed in love

I admit I may have seen better days, but I am still not to be had for the price of a cocktail – like a salted peanut.

Joseph Mankiewicz 1909–93

It is essential to have the confidence to know that someone out there is for you and that you will meet that person, even if you do encounter put-downs or disappointments along the way. This chapter is designed to bolster your confidence in your ability to succeed. When you have unshakeable confidence, as you will, it can propel you forward, giving you the strength to go on until you get precisely what you want.

The platform upon which unremitting confidence in any endeavour is built has three steps: (1) belief in yourself, (2) faith in what you have to offer, and (3) trust in your ability to succeed in your chosen enterprise. The exercises in the book so far have been designed to enable you to believe in yourself so you are now primed and ready to step up on to this confidence-boosting platform and increase your self-confidence to the point where you know that you will succeed in love.

The second step is faith in what you have to offer. Ask yourself, 'What is it that I have to offer a prospective partner?' Answer: you – the very person you have come to like and have faith in.

Do you have trust in your ability to succeed in your chosen enterprise? Well, even if we do have some work to do on this one, you have three major things very much in your favour. You have well and truly identified your chosen enterprise, which is love in the first degree, the noblest and most worthwhile endeavour of all. Furthermore, you have already demonstrated great interest and extraordinary determination to achieve magnificent twosome status by accessing this book and completing the exercises. Finally, and crucial to your ultimate success, you know you're up for this: you're not simply waiting for the person of your dreams to drop into your arms and stay there.

Now that we have agreed that you are qualified to stand on the platform of confidence, let's build greater confidence with a few simple but effective techniques. Before we do, I would like to dispel the myth that self-confident people are conceited. Self-confident people have their doubts and negative thoughts about themselves and their competence like the rest of us. It's just that they have the self-awareness to recognise these thoughts and replace them with positive alternatives. Do not make the mistake of confusing bragging with self-confidence; genuinely confident people do not need to bring attention to themselves or their accomplishments or denigrate other people, in order to feel good about themselves.

Whereas confident people expect success, those who are lacking in confidence are subconsciously setting themselves up for failure. They fear the worst and this fear creates a vicious circle of self-doubt, always ineffective and almost guaranteed to end in disappointment.

There is only one safe and sure way out of this vicious circle of self-doubt and that is to take things one step at a time. Now is the time to take a few more steps forward. You are already up there on the basic platform of confidence because you deserve to be. Greater self-confidence is best developed through a series of easily manageable chunk-size successes that build on one another.

To aim too high without first working through the intermediate steps is to risk returning to a cycle of failure and self-doubt. The intermediate steps to growing self-confidence are:

1 Overcoming your fears

2 Engaging in positive self-talk

3 Proper preparation

4 Visualising confidence

5 Avoiding the 'all-or-nothing' syndrome

6 Celebrating your achievements.

Let's take the steps one at a time.

1 Overcoming your fears

'Personality traits once thought to be the result of upbringing and experience are encoded in our human genes,' according to evidence from a unique project mapping the DNA of 10,000 people in Iceland. Scientists at DeCode, a 'gene mining' company based in Iceland, reported in October 2004 that they had identified the location of a gene that causes a fearful or anxious personality. This discovery perhaps heralds the prospect of future generations being genetically modified to eliminate unnecessary anxiety, but for those of us who are around now we will have to deal with our fears in order to overcome them.

The intelligent way to do this is to engage each of the following steps to confidence and to have fun, lots of fun, at the same time. It is all too easy to worry and become over-intense when participating in a programme of personal development, particularly, when the fruits of success are so appealing. To counter this intensity, take time out to enjoy yourself, preferably somewhere where you're likely to meet the sort of person you want to meet. Try worrying while you are laughing uncontrollably!

2 Engaging in positive self-talk

This is familiar territory for you because you already know that some of your most important conversations are the ones that you conduct with yourself. Self-talk governs your emotional state, which in turn affects your mental and physical wellbeing. You need to feel good in order to be confident and you won't grow in confidence if you keep doing yourself down. Be your greatest supporter! Give yourself frequent and realistically positive reassurances about how things should pan out. Be constructive in those one-sided private conversations that you have with yourself.

3 Proper preparation

You are preparing right now for the relationship of a lifetime by working your way steadily forward towards the Countdown. Don't be impatient! The chances are you still have some things to work on before you achieve ultimate success.

4 Visualising confidence

Visualisation is a type of meditation that involves using your imagination to help increase your confidence by seeing yourself achieve what you want to achieve in your mind's eye. Get yourself comfortable, relax, take a few deep breaths and picture a scenario that requires you to act with confidence – for example, meeting the person of your dreams in a crowded place and striking up a conversation. Use all your senses to set the scene and let the action develop, as you would wish to see it happen. Picture yourself acting confidently in all phases of the scenario, as if you were playing the starring role in a Hollywood movie. It worked for a B-movie actor who dreamed of becoming the president of the United States of America, Ronald Reagan, and it can work for your comparatively modest aspiration to meet Mr or Ms Absolutely Right.

5 Avoiding the 'all-or-nothing' syndrome

This is an all too common trap that perfectionists set for themselves. Unless the perfect outcome can be guaranteed from the outset, the perfectionist is reluctant to embrace what could be a life-changing experience, for fear of failing. The solution is to savour the chunk-size successes en-route to the big picture, to break down the steps to a winning outcome into individually manageable little adventures. Think about this book. It is not simply a grand statement of what you want to achieve. It is a series of manageable successes (chapters) leading progressively to the desired outcome.

6 Celebrating your achievements

Depending on the sort of difficulties you have encountered in relationships that went wrong and whether or not you have come to terms with them, some parts of *Countdown to Love* may present you with the occasional challenge. Give yourself the credit and the praise you deserve for having the grit to pick yourself up and give love another try!

These easy to handle guidelines, if you heed them, will help you to acquire greater confidence in your ability to succeed in love. You will find it becomes easier to say 'Yes' and 'No' with conviction, and you'll be better equipped to make the right choices in your relationships in the first place. You will attain a kind of freedom that may be new to you: the confidence to conduct your love life with the courage of your convictions.

 The Bottom Line

> Confident people expect success and that alone gives them a greater chance of finding it.

Appearance

*When a man opens the car door for his wife, it's
either a new car or a new wife.*

HRH Prince Philip, Duke of Edinburgh

I would not presume to tell you how to present yourself in public. You know what works for you and what doesn't. But we would probably agree that there are certain aspects to be taken care over and this chapter deals with my take on appearance. You will clearly place a different emphasis on some points but I hope that concentrating on these topics will help you to make the right decisions for you. We will briefly touch upon clothes, hair, make-up/male grooming, weight, smoking and posture.

But, first, why do these things matter and why is it so important to address them now? I believe you already know the answer to these questions. First impressions count for a lot and you, if you haven't already done so, are planning to meet your ideal partner ASAP.

I take advice from people who know what looks good on me. I met Tatiana, by chance, in a London street, when she stopped me to ask for directions. I must have looked well turned-out and, by implication, safe to talk to. Your ideal partner might walk into your life next week, so now is the perfect time to take a critical look at aspects of your appearance that perhaps you take for granted.

I know most of us, male and female alike, would love to look like someone from the cover of our favourite glossy magazine. But you must remember that models are always dieting to get into shape for the next picture shoot. He or she has been airbrushed by a computer graphics artist, had the skills of a make-up artist and expert hairdresser and the benefit of sympathetic lighting to help with definition and shape. To crown it all, the finger that clicked the shutter is attached to the crème de la crème of photographers, using the finest and most advanced equipment in the world.

This section is not intended to fool people into thinking that you are someone that you're not. The idea is to help you pinpoint and eliminate some of the classic errors of personal presentation that can get in the way of starting healthy new relationships. When you look good and feel great it's so much easier to relax and appear confident whenever you meet somebody who makes you go weak at the knees.

Clothes

The colour of your clothes speaks volumes about you but different colours suit different people, although there is no doubt that red has a special effect on most men. Many big department stores and some of the more enterprising boutiques employ personal shoppers with whom you can make a free appointment and get their advice on what colours and styles look good on you. Almost invariably, you'll be offered an appointment at a time when the store is not busy. You are usually under no obligation to buy, but, business being business, obviously they hope to win your custom. Some of my most successful shopping expeditions have been where experienced shop assistants have taken the time and trouble to select and colour co-ordinate outfits that look good especially on me. Remember to tell your personal shopper or the assistant specifically that you are not necessarily looking for the most fashionable or trendiest clothes, but for styles and colours that appear flattering on you.

The crime most perpetrated by men as they walk the earth searching for the perfect partner is to wear a pathetically cheap T-shirt with some nonsensical or anti-social message emblazoned across the front or back. It might have been all right for Bob Geldof but it's not all right for you. Every man, regardless of age, needs a classic T-shirt and it's worth shopping around to get the right one that makes the right statement about him. The same is true of jeans, trainers, well-polished shoes and, of course, a well-cut and skilfully chosen suit. An easy way of dressing that allows you to be comfortable and presentable at the same time is to wear a mix of smart and casual clothes.

Don't think you have to be impeccably dressed all the time, but bear in mind that love invariably strikes at some inconvenient or unexpected moment! Take your baggy old clothes and shiny suits down to the charity shop so that you can't wander around town ruining your chances of romance.

Hair

When a woman sees her reflection in the mirror is there anything more important to her than the look of her hair? Yet many women fail to grasp that most men like to have something soft and bouncy to play with and caress. The majority of women, once they hit 40, have a tendency to wear their hair shorter because their hairdresser tells them, or they read in a magazine, that short hair makes them look younger. This is not necessarily true; a lot depends on the shape of your face and the texture and condition of your hair. Surely it makes sense, if you're a woman looking for a man (not a woman) to love and adore you, to ask men, not women, what sort of hairstyle might suit you. If you prefer to take the easy option and rely on your hairdresser for advice, bear in mind that hairdressers are notorious for cutting hair short.

Men, women, are you one of the lucky ones? Have you found a talented hairdresser whom you can trust? If so, hang on to him or her. You are safe. Not everyone has such luck.

My advice is that unless you have your ideal crimper, beware! This is too important an area in which to cede power unless you are certain that you are receiving unbiased, professional advice on the most suitable hairstyle for you.

Men, if your hairdresser doesn't automatically attend to such details, ask them, when appropriate, to trim your eyebrows and any unsightly hairs protruding from your nose and ears while they have the scissors handy. Women generally don't approve of flyaway eyebrows and half-a-hedge protruding from each nostril, but they are much too polite to tell you. If you are losing your hair, wear it bristly short. If you have already lost it, capitalise on the fact that many women find a special sexiness in the shape of a man's head. Losing your hair certainly doesn't mean losing your sex appeal.

Make-up/male grooming
When it comes to women's make-up and male grooming, I am a great believer in being advised by the experts, unless you know precisely what suits you best. Customers can get tremendous value for money on trial products and free professional advice on what type of make-up flatters them and how best to apply it from most cosmetics counters within department stores. My sister works part-time on the make-up counter in a well-known provincial store and she was impressed with the in-depth training the cosmetics companies give their staff. The correct application of make-up is all-important, because men don't like to see a lot of make-up on women and wearing too much, especially heavy foundation, can make you look older.

Many men have discovered that grooming, particularly a facial scrub, improves the quality of their skin. Poor shaving technique leads to cuts, bumps, spots and redness, and subsequent shaves simply exacerbate the problem. The secret of a good shave is to lather the shaving soap into your skin with a shaving brush for a good two minutes before shaving. If you're using shaving cream or gel, it's worth paying a little extra for a good one. After shaving, add a touch of moisturiser, but be careful with your choice of aftershave lotion and apply it sparingly. Different fragrances suit different men and if you make the wrong choice, women have a tendency to notice. Seek the opinion of three women in your own age group (not your ex!) before settling on a new brand of aftershave. When you find one that does it for you, stick with it.

Weight

These days virtually anyone who is seriously overweight or obese can usually get a free 12-week course of treatment in England and Wales with Weight Watchers or Slimming World simply by making appointment with their GP. In the meantime, while you are slimming down, here are a few tips to get you ready for your next date:

Big boobs: The temptation is to dress over the chest completely, but this won't make it look any less dominant. A well-designed minimiser bra might suit you. V-neck tops and wrapover dresses work best, as they draw the eye downwards. Many men like big boobs!

Pear-shaped hips: Never wear a pencil skirt. Instead, choose a bias-cut fabric that will skim your curves, not cling to them. Over this soft base, you can lay a tailored jacket.

Big bum: Never wear jeans. Tailored, wide-leg trousers work best. Always choose a matt fabric and a top that covers your bottom and stomach, but not something that's clingy.

Chunky legs: Obviously mini-skirts and thick black tights are not the best look. Instead, go for longer-length dresses and skirts with an elegant, fluted cut. Trousers that are not too tight are another sensible option.

Overweight men: Long, free-flowing T-shirts and coats work well. Avoid jeans; opt for wide-legged trousers instead. Anything tailored will always be more slimming.

Smoking

Whether you choose to smoke or not is entirely up to you, but it is no longer regarded as cool or bright to smoke, and these days it is a substantial handicap to meeting potential partners, an increasing number of whom won't contemplate a date with a smoker. When I debated this point with a group of 50 or so potential *Countdown to Love* readers in north London – all of them, 30+, single and looking for a meaningful relationship – a staggering 65 per cent were immediately turned off by the idea of getting involved with someone who smokes. When I enquired if Mr or Ms Right might come with an occasional passion for recreational drugs, all but one person, a therapist, assured me that they certainly would not.

For 20 years, I was a chain-smoker. Then, almost 10 years ago, for no particular reason, I decided to quit. I have never smoked another cigarette and I no longer have any desire to do so. The secret to successful quitting? It's simple! No need for patches, potions, classes, hypnosis or gum. Just follow these three simple instructions to the letter:

1   Never put another cigarette in your mouth.

2   Never allow yourself to dwell on your craving for nicotine. As soon as you get the desire for a cigarette – and you will for months, or even years, to come – immediately change your thoughts. Do or think about something else but don't contemplate one single puff. It gets easier as the months go by.

3   Avoid intimate contact with anyone who smokes. One kiss can transfer enough nicotine on to your tongue to have you craving for more well into the next morning!

If you propose to quit using this straightforward and proven method, please reread and learn the instructions off by heart, never deviating from them – not even once – and bear in mind that you may need to eat less and exercise more because you might otherwise put on weight.

The change to your diet and exercise routine can in itself help to minimise cravings for tobacco and some recreational drugs. It's well worth investing in a 30-minute appointment with your dentist's hygienist because your teeth will stay whiter for longer without the yellowy-brown stain of nicotine. Good luck! You'll potentially double your chances of finding the ideal partner and you'll have oodles of spare cash!

Posture

Good posture gives the impression that you are both positive and self-assured. If you can maintain a good posture while looking relaxed – not stiff or dull – people will not only perceive you as more attractive and likeable, but successful and accomplished as well. Generally speaking, stomach in, back straight and head up is a good place to start.

A highly effective way to highlight and correct bad posture is to have a candid camera session with a friend. You can do this at home or outside on location. Film on to DVD or videotape for the convenience of instant playback and within the hour it will be blatantly obvious to you what you need to do to improve your posture and deportment.

 The Bottom Line

First impressions count for a lot. Take pride in your appearance.

CHAPTER 7

PART
2

Flirting

All our talents increase in the using, and every faculty both good and bad, strengthens by exercise.

Anne Brontë 1820–49

Flirting, if you are serious about meeting your ideal partner for a lasting relationship, is not a game, it is the starting grid where all great romances commence. The idea is to make the object of your affections aware of your presence, to intrigue, charm or captivate him or her before their interest evaporates or settles on someone else. What is obvious and striking about you will attract their attention at first, but you must follow up with something more potent than eye contact in order to make sparks fly and create a lasting impression. Plain women with handsome husbands and nondescript men with gorgeous wives know this.

As you contemplate, perhaps nervously, staking your claim to happiness with the person of your choice, bear in mind that the one you want is out there looking for someone to love at this very moment. The miracle is that you can be that someone when you tap into the Countdown philosophy. All you have to do at this stage is take the initiative and flirt when the opportunity arises, instead of looking the other way, hiding away in the background where nothing happens, or freezing like a deer when the spotlight shines on you.

Do not worry about the possibility of making a mistake, being rebuffed or making a fool of yourself in front of others. All these scenarios are possible but you will be adequately trained later in the book to handle disappointments so that you can pick yourself up and keep on going until you win in love. You will also be better equipped than you have ever been to screen out unsuitable suitors early, before they can make off with your heart.

A fear that many non-flirtatious people of all ages share (nearly always without foundation) is the belief that they are not handsome or beautiful enough to flirt with aplomb.

The next time you are out among a bunch of couples, take a good look at who's with whom. I would be surprised if you don't see some attractive women with men whose claim to fame is something other than their looks, and vice-versa. That's because beauty is in the eye of the beholder. Intelligent people who make a success of their relationships are more concerned with whether their partner is loyal, loving and lovely to be with than if he or she could double as an actor or a model.

When it comes to flirting, a number of factors come into play and we will explore these, but as a general rule most people find they are drawn to the person who acts in much the same way as they might do. This is because if two people react in a similar manner to a given situation, the chances are they going to understand each other and get along well. For instance, a woman at a party who is an extrovert is more likely to be attracted to blokes who look as though they're having a great time, while a quiet bloke is more likely to appeal to a woman who is shy. This flies in the face of the notion that opposites attract. Certainly, they do, but they don't necessarily get on famously in the long term unless they also have a tremendous amount in common.

The essential thing to know about human nature in order to be able to flirt with confidence is that most of us take notice of and feel attracted to those people who show a genuine interest in us.

Doesn't your heart skip a beat when you catch someone looking at you across a crowded room? We are susceptible to this kind of personal attention because it makes us feel special. Who do you usually smile at? The person who smiles at you first, of course!

People, like mirrors, are naturally reflective. More often than not, the way we feel about others is a reflection of the way they think about us. If we believe that someone is taking a genuine interest in us, we tend to feel kindly towards him or her, we feel drawn towards them. When someone ignores us or if we suspect that they dislike us, don't we just hate them? Many of our attitudes and patterns of behaviour towards other people are determined by the way they treat us first, so if you have any hang-ups about becoming a flirt, now is the time to review your rationale. No one will admire you for being a wallflower.

Showing interest in another person invariably means being the *first* to smile, being the first to make eye contact, being the first to introduce yourself and being the first to spark a conversation. All you need is the courage to take the first step. The next time you encounter someone who strikes you as future partner potential, don't hesitate, take the initiative: flirt!

How? Well, you could start with a smile, that invariably smoothes the way and makes everything much easier, but you already know that. I prompted you to smile on occasions like this in a previous chapter (see page 51).

What next? Eye contact! Looking straight into someone's eyes has a powerful effect on that person. Some people, particularly women, have a tendency to look downwards or away when they detect the unexpected attentions of a stranger. This does not mean bad news. Only if the object of your desire fails to look back at you within 45 seconds, should you consider that your attentions might not be welcome.

Next? Body language! Your posture, your poise, the expression on your face, the angle of your head, the position of your hands, all combine to communicate more about you than anything you're likely to say in the first minute or two of conversation, unless, of course, you have a surprise to offer.

What comes next? It's noddy time! If your gaze is returned within 45 seconds, give that person a respectful nod. That nod is code for, 'Can I come closer?' Don't wait for a response. Move within talking range and say something. If the object of your desire is a woman and she is among a group of other women, the chances are that they will very inconveniently engage themselves in conversation as you approach.

Fear not! Destiny favours the bold. Stand directly in front of the chosen one but leave at least one metre of personal space between the two of you and politely wait for a pause in the conversation. Don't be intimidated because you are outnumbered. If you're not wanted, they will make that clear, but the woman you were aiming for will admire you for your audacity. On the other hand, your attentions might be very welcome.

What on earth am I going to say? Anything that comes into your head! 'Hi,' will do for a start, and you might want to introduce yourself by name. A hand outstretched ready to be shaken, complete with a name, is difficult to ignore! One important thing to bear in mind at this point is that people have a habit of categorising new faces based on their first impressions. So, if you start the conversation by complaining about the music, you run the risk of being labelled a moaner, whereas if you manage to charm your newfound acquaintance, you will be regarded as charming until such time as you prove otherwise. It is perfectly okay for men or women to make the first move!

The Bottom Line

Flirting with someone, who turns out to be emotionally and physically available, leads to lust...

CHAPTER 8

PART
2

Lust

When she raises her eyelids, it's as if she were
taking off all her clothes.

Colette 1873–1954

The first indicator of love to manifest itself when you meet someone who makes sparks fly and your flesh tingle is lust. The sheer excitement and unparalleled exhilaration of someone new in your life sets off a powerful cocktail of chemicals that rage seemingly out of control in your brain and you convince yourself (not difficult, when you want to believe) that he or she must be 'the one'.

Lust is an integral part of love, but it is the cause of much distress and misunderstanding in the complex domain of romance because it also fuels one-night stands, baby-making and a host of well meaning but hopelessly impractical liaisons that are destined to end in break-up and tears. In terms of its potential to cause untold misery in the world, only war and famine are more potent in the grief stakes.

Lust, unless potential lovers are balanced and fully prepared for the delicate task of choosing the right partner, can lead to a false start. It is for this reason that I have positioned this chapter on lust here although the search for your ideal partner does not even begin until Part 4 of the book.

In this chapter, I am simply going to alert you to what can and often does go wrong when your brain gets all fired up with lust because you mastered the art of flirting and hit lucky with a potential new partner. Of course, it is quite possible that this individual is the right one for you, but statistically it's odds against. When we progress to the real thing, a few chapters along the line, we will learn how to handle lust in all of its many guises so that we end up with the appropriate partner for a happy and lasting relationship, instead of getting side-tracked by a delicious no-hoper.

Love starts with lust, but that all-consuming feeling of raw passion can only last for a few hours, a few days or a few weeks at that insatiable level of intensity, assuming that the lovers in question are freely available to consummate their relationship and are not parted. This is because nature's prime objective is to link men and women together under the influence of a powerful hormonal cocktail that causes them to procreate, not think!

Next, comes infatuation, which can last anything from five minutes to a year or two, and then something gentler, less intense, called attachment takes over when the chemical rush has subsided. We now begin to see our partner, perhaps, for the first time, in their true colours and some of those little habits that we found so endearing when we were lusting after them now seem downright irritating. The notion that love is blind takes on a whole new meaning for you when you finally realise that you are living with the wrong partner.

After attachment (unless you have established a wonderful relationship with the right partner, which is the premise of the Countdown philosophy) comes disenchantment. This increasingly disagreeable phase can span any period from the night of the wedding to the moment that the pain and disillusionment becomes unbearable and the warring parties split up.

Love does not have to be like this, as all the magnificent twosomes that have contributed to this book and many more know to their great personal satisfaction and joy. Lust, on a calmer and more controlled level, can last forever if both parties to a meaningful relationship have taken the trouble to choose each other with care and to nurture the relationship so that it can survive any trial.

For long-term relationships to flourish, qualities like thoughtfulness, generosity, self-assurance and a sense of purpose, together with physical warmth, decency, humour, the ability to listen and to express affection, are substantial ingredients in the matchmaking mix. Sexiness and the ability to blow each other's brains out when your lover succumbs to your carnal desires is, of course, a momentous consideration, but, if you want the relationship to go on forever, it should not be the primary basis on which you choose your partner.

 ## The Bottom Line

> Lust is a legitimate part of love, but a
> dangerous one.

PART 3

Before Lighting the Touch Paper

If anything can go wrong, it will, and at the most inopportune time.

Murphy's Law

CHAPTER 1

PART
3

Friends or assassins?

My dear, she's been my greatest friend for fifteen years.
I know her through and through, And I tell you that
she hasn't got a single redeeming quality.

W Somerset Maugham 1874–1965

Okay, so we bought the book, and we wholeheartedly mean to find Mr or Ms Absolutely Right or make a resounding success of the relationship that we already have. What could possibly go wrong?

A threat uncomfortably close to home, perhaps? Do you honestly believe that every single one of your trusted friends wants you to be blissfully happy in your magnificent twosomeness-to-come? Happier and more contented than they are?

Let's put it another way. Have you ever been envious of one of your friends? Have you ever been tempted to stick a spanner in the works to protect the status quo because, secretly, you don't want them moving on and leaving you behind? If you can honestly answer, 'No,' you would be naïve to think that everyone is as noble as you are.

Some people will stop at nothing to protect what they see as an idyllic friendship, one in which you serve to massage their ego with your constant trials and disappointments, in return for which they will comfort you and listen to your woes. 'Friends' like this can have difficulty in handling your successes and may be instrumental in prolonging your tenure as a singleton. Behind the scenes, with little manoeuvres and the things they say, they may even prevent you from having a relationship.

Jealousy within friendships is often the main cause of difficulties when a new lover enters your life, especially when you announce that this one is the one! Best friends can feel neglected and pushed out by this new special person in your life and your lover may feel resentful of people who have known you for so much longer than he or she has. Friends who feel threatened by the turn of events can magnify any problems that arise between you and your partner by taking your side and coming between the two of you at times when the relationship is under pressure.

Of course, your friends will probably be salt-of-the-earth types and absolutely genuine, not the type to gossip or whisper behind your back, but it is worth satisfying yourself on this point before you spontaneously introduce your new beloved. Historically, friends are more likely to stick the knife into your back or commit treason against you than a complete stranger is. And how might they justify their actions if you catch them red-handed giving the low-down on you to the person you love so much, you would die for? 'Oh, I felt it was my duty to say something: after all, I know you only too well!'

I have known Frayne since our teens when we were flatmates in Notting Hill and we have quite a history. My first wife Valerie was originally his girlfriend. There can be no denying the fact that I plotted to steal her and marry her. However, this story does not concern my misdemeanours, it relates to his skulduggery the very first time he had a moment alone with Tatiana. In the true spirit of the chapter title, I shall throw him to the wolves in front of your eyes, secure in the knowledge that, despite his well-deserved embarrassment, we will always be friends.

After a very enjoyable dinner and get-together with Tatiana and Frayne in a village pub, just outside Cambridge, I returned towards the dining table, just in time to overhear Frayne saying, most emphatically, as I approached from behind his back. 'Don't get involved, Tatiana. Believe me, I know him. He'll just walk out and dump you the moment it suits him!'

For those of you who say you reap what you sow, I say, how innocent are you?

You must purge any negative influences and triggers from within your network of friends. Stop interacting with people who are not supportive of your quest for the ideal partner, people who facilitate your single status and that includes, of course, any ex who has an unhealthy emotional hold over you. Stay loyal to your friends of many years' standing, of course, but spend quality time with people who are headed in the same direction as you are. Make friends with people who have a positive direction to their lives – or are working towards one – because you could find them enormously stimulating and rewarding to be with.

As a direct result of the exercises you completed in Parts 1 and 2 of the book, you will know that the best way to build significant relationships in your life – with a loved one, family, friends or workmates – is to become your own best friend first. The more you believe in and respect yourself, the more others will believe in and respect you. The more attractive you feel on the inside, the more this will be reflected on the outside and within the circle of friends in which you move. Before you look for the qualities that you admire in others, think about what you can do to adopt those admirable qualities yourself.

Our lives are enriched and broadened (and humbled at times) by the idiosyncrasies of our various friends. Anaïs Nin, the French-born American writer of novels and short stories (1903–77), observed that *'Each friend represents a world in us, a world possibly not born until they arrive, and it is only by this meeting that a new world is born.'*

Quite apart from the thrill, the excitement and the sheer pleasure of their company, there is the reassurance and contentment of simply being among friends that is an integral part of their tried and tested companionship. Many of us, I feel sure, have done many things (not all of which are to be recommended) that we would never have dreamed of doing if it were not for one or other of our friends.

Prepare your friends in advance for any impending changes you intend to make in your private life because good friends will always be friends and you will want to keep them for a lifetime, faults and all. Once you have convinced yourself that they are truly worthy of your trust, take them into your confidence, talk things over frankly with them, so that when the time comes and you meet your ideal partner you carry your friends with you into this new adventure.

The Bottom Line

I'll get by with a little help from my friends, but friends can be lethal when you meet 'the one'.

Self-sabotage

What other dungeon is so dark as one's own heart!
What jailer so inexorable as one's self!

Nathaniel Hawthorne 1804–64

People who genuinely want a loving relationship (and those who think they do, but are deceiving themselves) sabotage their dreams in many different ways. Knowingly or unknowingly, they make sure that romance never happens for them. In this chapter, let's look at some of the most common forms of self-sabotage.

If you should feel, while reading, that any of these conditions relate specifically to you, later in Part 3 there will be an opportunity to access proven self-healing strategies or, in the case of depression, to be referred to a reliable source of alternative relief. Interestingly, whereas some people can live their entire lives without realising that they are responsible for their own unhappiness, others, when they recognise the telltale signs of their dysfunctional behaviour in print or in therapy, are positively shocked into action, breaking out of their self-imposed prison.

The six primary aspects of self-sabotage:
1 Desperation
2 Psychological damage from childhood

3 Emotional injury from a previous relationship
4 Excess baggage
5 Depression
6 Guilt.

Desperation

Whenever you're desperate for anything, no matter what it is you want, desperation shows in your eyes, in your body language and in the words you use and the tone of voice in which you speak. If you're a woman over 35 looking for a lifelong partner, understandably, you may well have a sense of urgency because your biological clock is ticking away and this is important should you want to start a family. In relationship matters, desperation is the kiss of death to any impending romance, which is why, before you seriously embark on your search for Mr or Ms Absolutely Right in future chapters, I shall encourage you to take a relaxed but highly organised approach to your dating.

I don't need to remind you about the tortoise and the hare and who got there first, but I do find I have to constantly impress on would-be romantics that the easy-going, calm and controlled approach in pursuit is more appealing to the opposite sex. Whenever you feel desperate for immediate results, get your trainers on and go for a jog. The only thing you will feel desperate for when you get back is breath! Incidentally, jogging (keep it gentle if you're not used to it) is great for working off anxiety.

Psychological damage from childhood

Damage from childhood might seem a delicate choice of heading to include in such an insensitive theme as self-sabotage, but when you get right down to it, we are all responsible as adults for making the best of our lives, no matter what has happened in the past.

The impelling memory I carry forward from my stress management consultancy is that those who are determined or inspired to overcome a problem will, and those who cannot or will not face up to reality, no matter how difficult or unjust the situation, will remain victims. This is so sad because there is someone out there who wants to nurture and love that person, but first he or she must do whatever it takes to make themselves loveable. If that person is you, this book is your vehicle for a well-deserved leap forward in life; a genuine opportunity to learn how to win the love you want. I know it's not easy, I was once where you are now.

Emotional injury from a previous relationship

The ex phenomenon is the subject of a whole chapter that comes later. Most of us, battle-scarred, angry and confused, after a period of convalescence and mourning, manage to pick ourselves up from the break-up, dust ourselves down and emerge wiser and more determined to get it right next time. If this sounds like you, then in all probability you're coping as well or better than most people are. We will deal with your specific needs later because it would be inappropriate and wrong (in most cases, but not all) to include you among the self-saboteurs.

This piece is directed at the hard core of good, honest and hard-working men and women, some of them single parents, others heartbroken dads who don't get to see their kids as much as they would like, who swear they will never love again and they mean it. Therein lies the anomaly of writing this piece, because they won't be reading this or any other relationship book. They have given up completely on the romantic side of life, some because their hearts have been wrenched apart so cruelly that they dare not love again.

Only their close family, their real friends and caring workmates who know them well have any chance of bringing them round. I can't do it in a book they won't read, and, in any event, it will take more than a book. They have had the emotion sucked out of them by a relationship into which they invested all of their love and trust and their partner betrayed them. These people know they genuinely didn't deserve the treatment they got.

Are they entirely blameless? No, because they committed the most fundamental romantic breach of all: they fell in love with someone who, in the event, turned out to be wrong for them. If only they could be persuaded to try again, this time with the benefit of hindsight and the Matchmaking Equation to guide them towards the right choice, the chances are they would make someone the ideal partner.

Excess baggage

This a catch-all for anything that may not transfer smoothly from one (or no) relationship to another. This includes your hang-ups, all six kids, the Alsatian and your geriatric mother in the attic upstairs, complete with her talking parrot.

Obviously, you will need to give a lot of thought to your particular situation and the individual responsibilities that you have. Kids are so important and they warrant a chapter of their own, which comes later. All you need to bear in mind now is that the burden of your children, your barking dog, ailing mother or screaming parrot are no reason to sell yourself short in the relationship stakes.

To some people, a prospective partner with responsibilities is an extremely attractive prospect; to others, not. Baggage means different things to different people. Generally, nightmare-type baggage requires working out in the chapters to come so that it can't cause damage in a future relationship, whereas personal baggage generated by a passion for living and the difficulties of life demonstrate vitality and are regarded by many as plus or non-negative factors.

Depression

Depression, like the common cold, is an illness that can affect anyone, including the rich, the famous and the happily in love. One in five of us will be affected by the condition at some stage in our lives. It is the experience of everyone who has suffered from depression that depressive episodes frequently vary in their intensity and these episodes may come and go for no apparent reason. The initial part of the depressive phase is usually of a reasonably slow onset, but in some more serious cases of depression, individuals can find themselves engulfed in gloom and despondency without warning and for no apparent reason.

As depression creeps up on us by stealth and silently takes over, many of us tend to soldier on bravely with our usual way of life, denying to ourselves and to others that anything is a matter with us. We battle on as best we can, oblivious to the reality that the joy of life is gradually being squeezed out of us. Our friends try to help us, but most of the time they just can't reach us because we are somewhere that they are not.

Depression, in all its various degrees and forms, is too complex a subject to discuss in detail here. Many self-saboteurs ruin their chances of finding or developing a meaningful relationship by ignoring the warning symptoms of gloom, feelings of inadequacy and difficulty in concentrating, by not seeking help or effective treatment. Most (but not all) forms of non-clinical depression are treatable without specialist intervention and many can be remedied without anti-depressants or multi-session therapy.

A clear understanding of the root cause of an individual's depression is the obvious starting point for recovery, but it is unrealistic to imagine that sufferers will be in a fit condition to figure this out for themselves – no matter how intelligent they may be. The problem is often exacerbated because many people, particularly men, are ashamed to admit that they are depressed. Depression, although frightening, is never permanent. It does not reduce our value as human beings, but it does need treatment.

Without wishing to appear commercial on a subject that I know brings untold misery to millions of Britons every year, the best advice I can give to anyone who feels depressed is to read a book on the subject that I wrote to help myself – it worked! *Beat*

Depression is published by Hodder and Stoughton and judging by the number of thank-you letters and e-mails I receive from readers – some of which would probably reduce you to tears of happiness at their recovery – I have no doubt it can work for you.

Guilt

Guilt is anger directed inwardly at ourselves and it's a high price to pay for not taking a compassionate and forgiving look at the reality of our lives. Whenever we feel guilty we get agitated and angry, either for doing something we shouldn't have done or for not doing something we should have done.

It's an extremely immobilising and debilitating game that we play with ourselves and the self-punishment we dish out and inflict on our ego becomes harsher and more admonishing with every repeated occurrence. For what: a moment of stupidity, a mistake, for falling short of expectations, for acting like the fallible human being that indeed we are? The fact is that honest, decent people feel more guilt than those who don't care. Why should we beat ourselves up with such cruel ferocity? Aren't we just doing the best we can now, with a view towards doing better in future?

Anxiety in the form of fear/self-harm/bulimia/anorexia etc can take hold over us as a direct result of feeling guilty. We begin to feel afraid of situations in which we might fail to live up to our personal expectations. We are afraid of what we might do to ourselves if we fail again. We are afraid of own anger. We avoid new opportunities, new people, new situations and new challenges. Predictably, we enter a rut and then feel guilty because we aren't doing more for ourselves. In a worse case scenario, some people become incapacitated by guilt, afraid of doing anything in case they 'let themselves down' again, or they set about doing things to destroy what little self-esteem they have left.

This vicious cycle of negative energy – from one part of our brain to the other – can have devastating effects. It poisons relationships, inhibits personal growth, stifles expansion of your horizons and torpedoes the attainment of your goals. Also, it hurts. Guilt is that uncomfortable feeling that immobilises you, now, as a result of something that has or hasn't happened in the past, while worry is the contrivance that preoccupies you at the most important time of your life, now, about something that may or may not happen in the future. Remorse for something that did or did not happen yesterday, and dread of what may or may not happen tomorrow, is no way to live your life and it doesn't offer a cat in hell's chance of delivering the loving partner you seek.

If you recognise yourself here and you are serious about wanting a permanent relationship, you will need to learn how to come to terms with guilt, internalised anger and worry, in order to manage it or work it out of your system. We shall make a start in a chapter titled *Releasing the venom*. We will succeed, of course, but it won't necessarily be a piece of cake, so expect to work, not just read.

The Bottom Line

Are you in this chapter? If so, we'll get things sorted. Recognition is part of the battle won.

CHAPTER 3

PART
3

The ex phenomenon

'Tis better to have loved and lost
Than never to have loved at all.

Alfred, Lord Tennyson 1809–92

Some couples part amicably, as my first wife and I did, and it's a pleasure, not a challenge, to meet them and their new partner in a chance encounter. Others, like the ending of my second marriage, can be brutal and test us to the limit.

This chapter does not concern itself with those relationships that end agreeably. It deals exclusively with the potentially troublesome ex who can't or won't accept that it's time to move on. In essence, they need to be convinced that it's over, that you both need a clean break to restructure your lives and to prepare yourselves emotionally and practically for the right relationship when the time comes.

Which ex are you? Are you the one who's getting out? Or are you the person who's been dumped or duped but you haven't come to terms with things yet and you're still desperately hoping it will all come together again?

Let's look at things first from the perspective of the person who is ending the relationship.

With some people you need to be as firm and unyielding as steel. With others (who may be extremely vulnerable), you need to be as firm and unyielding as steel, but also caring and compassionate in the manner that you convey the message that it's over. Likewise, in the immediate aftermath of the split.

Obviously, things become more complicated if your ex is or was your spouse, and also when children are involved, but the best way to fend off a persistent ex and get them to realise that the relationship is over is to stick rigidly to the dos and don'ts that follow. They might strike you as being a bit stark and clinical, as indeed they are, but like most efficient functions, they are designed to get the desired result. Clearly, it would be helpful to the dispossessed if you manage your affairs in a humane and decent manner:

Do:

- ✔ Refuse all offers of dates, favours and 'innocent' get-togethers

- ✔ Bluntly and unequivocally express your wish to be left alone

- ✔ Make sure that your body language reinforces your message

- ✔ Look your ex straight in the eye when speaking and don't kiss or touch

- ✔ Agree the ground rules for fair and proper access to the kids

- ✔ Make it plain if contact is unavoidable that you have moved on and there is no going back

- ✔ Return all of your ex's belongings, ideally via a parcel delivery firm or friends

- ✔ Inform your family, friends and workmates (if appropriate) that it's over

✔ Confirm to your ex's family, friends and workmates (if they contact you) that it's over

✔ Contact your solicitor for specific advice and guidance if children or property are involved and/or you are being intimidated, badly treated or starved of money to which you/your children are entitled.

Don't:

✗ Give your ex the opportunity to manipulate you

✗ Mention the good times you had together in the past

✗ Use the kids as weapons

✗ Reply to cards, letters or e-mails or return calls, except where children are involved.

On that final point, there is one significant variation in procedure where school-age children are involved in the break-up. The Children's Act states that the interests of the child are paramount so you should both co-operate in attending parent/teacher evenings and responding to requests from the head teacher for parents to contact the school. Be courteous but emotionless with your ex when discharging these obligations. No drinks 'for old time's sake'.

If things should turn nasty, you may have to:

● Inform your family, friends and workmates

● Protect your credit cards, bank accounts and other financial assets

● Change your door lock, telephone number and mobile number, if appropriate

● Carry your mobile with you at all times

● Consult a solicitor

- Threaten to call the police and be prepared to do so if necessary
- Move in with one of your friends for a while
- Take a holiday
- Move location permanently.

When you stick rigidly to these well-tried and tested guidelines the ex phenomenon becomes much easier to work through and handle not only for you, but also for your ex as well. Admittedly, there will always be a toxic minority of desperate and unreasonable exes who resort to guerrilla tactics. They fail to respect your privacy, they become time and energy vampires in a selfish bid to prevent you from establishing or enjoying a new relationship; and when you do meet your ideal partner, they try to use guilt to drive a wedge between the two of you. But they won't succeed, because in the next chapter you're about to learn a new technique to neutralise their efforts and release the venom.

Now to the deserted ex, the one who has been dumped, the understandably distraught and lost individual who is still in love with someone from the past. The antidote to this condition is the same for those who have been duped (perhaps, by someone who you now know to be married or otherwise emotionally unavailable for a lasting relationship with you). You too can be rescued by the techniques that follow.

You may think that I have been heavy handed and insensitive to your feelings so far in this chapter, but I believe the most decent thing any departing ex can do is to be honest with you. Truth is like a sword that cuts through and sets you free. It hurts like hell to be on the receiving end of such truth, but the alternative, if time is allowed to drift by before reality dawns, will be more penetrating and crueller in the end, as I, myself, discovered at my father's funeral.

My mother, now in her 80s, handled my father's funeral with dignity and remarkable generosity of heart. I knew all the guests except one – an elderly woman who I had never seen before. She didn't mingle with the family. She was a solitary figure standing well back on the periphery. 'Who's that?' I asked my mother. My sister flashed me an anxious look, but it was too late, the words were out. 'A retired head teacher,' was the eventual response. 'She's waited 50 years for your father to leave me and marry her. Of course, he never did. I'll go and have a chat with her, she must be feeling awful.'

We understand that we have to get things sorted. The action plan that follows is based on an elementary but powerful stress management technique that is suitable for self-application. If you follow the instructions and use it you will succeed in eliminating any errant lover from your life. It never fails. There is no one in the world who can't be eliminated from your life using this method.

All we have to do to free you from the emotional wilderness of your ex is to change the default settings of your mind (your automatic thought pattern known as the conditioned reflex) so that you no longer continue to dwell on or yearn for him or her. If this sounds puzzling, let me assure you that it's not cutting-edge science, it's the easiest technique in the book!

The Russian physiologist who deserves the credit for this system is the Nobel Prize winner, Ivan Petrovich Pavlov (1849–1936). The most famous of Pavlov's experiments were his studies on the behaviour of dogs. He would ring a bell and then feed the dogs. He repeated this procedure many times over a period of weeks: he rang the bell, the dogs salivated and ate the food. After a time, the dogs would salivate at the sound of the bell – even when no food was available. Pavlov described their response to the bell as a conditioned reflex: bell, salivation, food.

This type of reaction – responding instantaneously to a stimulus – became known as the Pavlovian response and it was the source of Pavlov's insights into human behaviour. Our basic human thought processes, Pavlov found, work in much the same way and this is why it is sometimes necessary to revise the default settings of our minds, that is to say, the stimulus that sets us off thinking the same old things, time after time.

When we hear the bell, we don't want to salivate when no food is forthcoming. Likewise, when we think about our ex, we don't want to yearn for this person when they're not there for us any more. As humans, we can make ourselves aware that such stimuli are self-defeating and false, that we do not have to make the conditioned response. To break the power of the association with your ex, I invite you to use a basic technique from stress management. You'll need one piece of equipment – a rubber band! Unbelievable maybe, but that's all you need.

Losing in love is almost guaranteed to induce anger, depression and despair; all these emotions combine to make up the ex phenomenon. You may feel that you will never love or be loved again. You will, of course, but you cannot be expected to believe this on day one of the therapy that I'm going to prescribe for you. The overwhelming sense of shock, outrage, disbelief and heart-rending grief at losing your lover defies all rational thought. It shatters the very bedrock of your emotions. Because you are already hurting so much, I have no qualms about introducing you to yet more pain – aversion therapy – in the form of a rubber band to be worn around at the wrist at all times, day and night, for a period of 30 days.

Make sure it fits loosely enough not to restrict circulation, but snugly enough so it won't fall off. Every time you think of your ex, snap the rubber band! Snap it firmly so that it stings, but not hard enough to leave welts on your wrist.

This type of aversion therapy might seem crazy but it works. How does it work? Your subconscious mind quickly comes to associate the twang of pain from the rubber band with thoughts of the offending ex-lover. Your subconscious mind will, over time, short-circuit the thought process to avoid the pain. As long as you never forget to twang, four or five weeks of this treatment is usually all you need to banish even the most invasive ex from mind. Thoughts of your ex become less and less frequent and soon it will be time to cast off the rubber band and celebrate your new-found freedom with champagne and friends.

The Bottom Line

Be aware of the dos and don'ts of breaking-up. Use a rubber band and your ex is history.

Releasing
the venom

There were three of us in this marriage, so it was a bit crowded.

Diana, Princess of Wales, 1961–97

Now that we have decided to move on and find lasting happiness with the right partner in the very near future, it's time, once and for all, to deal with any unhelpful, negative or destructive feelings: no matter whether they stem from childhood, the behaviour of your ex, any previous exes or the man in the moon. If we really intend to be sorted, to prepare ourselves for magnificent twosomeness in the future, we need to deal with any demons from the past, here and now. In this chapter and the next we do.

If you are a happy, well-balanced individual with no hang-ups and no debilitating baggage to import into a new relationship and spoil it, please skip this chapter.

Many of us need help and guidance in acknowledging and then letting go of the unpleasant, traumatic, pent-up emotions associated with the past, regardless of their origination. Clearly, this has the potential to be a rewarding chapter, though not necessarily an enjoyable one, so why should we participate in the exercises, assuming that they apply to us?

I advise participants to view it as their insurance policy against fouling up in a future relationship, their own precautionary emotional health check not unlike the MOT you have done on your car, or the scanning device you run on your computer for bugs. They're all safeguards for the future.

It would be a shame, once you find your ideal partner, if the relationship was to go pear-shaped because you were not emotionally fit and ready; if something bad from the past was holding you in its grasp, threatening your future. This chapter is designed to drain the energy-sapping power of sad or traumatic events so that the sting is taken out of the associated emotion, neutralising it. It enables you to process feelings of anguish and betrayal after being rejected, dumped, or humiliated in some way, and it can be effective in negating the influences of dominant personalities.

Obviously, if you have a psychiatric or psychological problem requiring medical attention or one-to-one therapy, specialist treatment is what you need and you should not proceed with this chapter without professional advice. The basic stress management formulations put forward here are beneficial to all people with non-diagnosable psychological problems and hang-ups and that generally includes most readers and 95 per cent of adults attending for counselling with emotional or relationship-related problems.

Whether you are a man or woman, don't pretend that you're stronger or less hurt than you really are. There is no shame in being a victim; there is no shame in being dumped or abandoned – it happens to the most beautiful, talented and worthy people. As we progress, give yourself time and space to let go of whatever emotions need to be released. Let the tears flow or thump a cushion if you feel angry or confused. Try not to judge your emotions or let anyone else judge them as they emerge. Very often we are surprised by our emotions – we may feel anger when we think we should be sad or vice versa. If you have trouble in physically expressing any emotion at all, try writing about what has happened, or draw or paint a picture symbolising the dilemma you are dealing with.

In order to move on from trauma, freeing our pent-up emotions so that we can make the best of an existing or a brand-new relationship, we need to pass through three distinct but overlapping phases. Some people have the ability to pass through these phases almost without noticing, while for others it's tough. The first distinctive phase is shock/denial; the second is anger/guilt (sometimes accompanied with depression); and the third and final phase, which is where we aim to end up the morning after you have completed the next chapter, is understanding/acceptance.

I suspect I am right in thinking that if we have some work to do here, you have already – perhaps a long time ago or maybe more recently – been through the shock/denial phase. We will pick up on anger/guilt (earned or unearned guilt – it doesn't matter which; all that matters is that we get rid of it) and move on to understanding/acceptance ASAP.

It may be that you are not in the right mood now to tackle this chapter, which is not an easy one for some people. That's okay, just read, and some other time when you are feeling in the right frame of mind to tackle the exercises, you can do them at your own pace. Different people release pent-up emotions at different rates. Take care not to overdo the release. You may need to let go of your emotions gradually, over a longer period, rather than all at once, which suits the majority of people and is my preferred option.

Before we get started, I should point out that I am presupposing that you know exactly what or who it is that is causing you to feel emotionally distressed – if indeed that is how you feel. If you often feel emotionally distressed, but you genuinely don't know why, it is most likely that you are being affected by a dominant personality. This person could be dead or alive and will be someone who exerted a strong influence over you at some time in your life. This has nothing to do with the supernatural or the occult, it simply means that the control they exercised over you in the past is having an unfortunate influence on you now.

To get to the therapeutic starting post, you must correctly identify the dominant personality. This is very easy to do. Simply get pen and paper and write the name of every person who has opposed you or abused you in some way from infancy to the present day. A typical list might start with your mother, father, grandmother, stepfather and nanny... right through to your present boss or your ex.

Make sure your list is complete. Now go through the list and strike off the person who affects you the least. You must strike off only one name at a time. For instance, if you have 20 names on your list, you must go through the list 19 times striking off the person who affects you the least from the names now remaining on the list. When you're done, you are left with only one name, and this is the dominant personality who is affecting you now. Now you can proceed to the therapeutic starting post to discharge the influence they have over you.

Releasing the venom is a very private ritual that involves giving up your grievances and getting to grips with the basics of anger management so that you can harness the emotive power of anger and recycle it to fuel your immediate and future happiness.

The process is straightforward and virtually everybody can do it as long as they are serious about moving on to a brighter, happier future. The rewards of accomplishing the exercises in this chapter and the next are all beneficial; there is no downside except, perhaps, a private flood of tears.

In common with just about anyone who has suffered any form of trauma, after a period of shock/denial, I felt angry and guilty about being partly paralysed by stroke. Although it took me some time to summon up the guts to give it a go, instead of allowing my anger/guilt (smoking/rich foods/binge drinking/unhealthy lifestyle

= hypertension/stroke) to ferment, I harnessed the emotive power of anger to fuel the writing of a book called *After Stroke*. This, in effect, was my passport to getting better and now you too can use this seven-step stress management system to come to terms with the past and revitalise your prospects for the future.

I call it releasing the venom and it works like this:

1   **Sit** yourself down comfortably and alone in front of a mirror and admit frankly to yourself what's wrong.

2   **Work** off your anger and guilt. Make sure you have pillows and handkerchiefs to hand.

3   **Decide** what, if anything, can be done to put things right and, if possible, immediately do it. If this works, go straight to step 6, if not, progress to step 4 .

4   **Reframe** the problem area.

5   **Focus** on the future, not the past.

6   **Sacrifice** your misery.

7   **Forgive** yourself and everyone else.

If you're in the mood, let's get started.

Sit down

Sit yourself down comfortably and alone in front of a mirror. Make sure there are no distractions by switching off the radio or TV, taking the telephone off the receiver and muting your mobile. If you're likely to be interrupted by others, now is not a good time to do this exercise. If conditions are right and you have a mind to succeed, admit frankly to yourself what's wrong. Look yourself straight in the eye and acknowledge the problem no matter how awful or trivial it might seem. Do not attach or allocate blame. Verbalise the problem and watch yourself saying what's wrong. Now, using no more than six words to capture the main thrust of the problem, say those words out loud and repeat them three times, looking at yourself while you speak.

Work off your anger

Work off your anger and guilt. This is definitely the time for amateur dramatics. Make sure you have a pillow handy to pummel as you work through your anger and hostility at the situation that you find yourself in. Hankies are handy to have around too because some people find that tears come flooding out with the spent emotion. I would like you to try this. Sit quietly, close your eyes and relax, with pillow and hankies to hand. Imagine yourself alone in an empty, dimly lit courtroom.

You are the judge and jury in this courtroom. You have absolute power of discretion in deciding guilt or otherwise and you alone, sitting upright in the judge's wooden chair, will pass sentence on the guilty and carry out or oversee the punishment. Now, in your mind's eye, see the person who has hurt you being brought into the dock before you. Imagine yourself dealing with them, as you think fit.

In your idea of a perfect world, what would they have to do or suffer to earn your forgiveness? Imagine the scene happening now, play it through in your mind, enjoy it, savour it. Remember this is your court. You can do anything you like. Keep going, until you have worked out your wrath and resentment in your mind's eye and on the pillow, if necessary. If you're a person who has difficulty visualising in your mind, write, draw, or paint your ideal scenario for justice. When you're done, open your eyes and look in a mirror. Tell yourself that the time for blame and retribution has come and gone. You're moving on to a real-world solution.

Some people need the professional touch of a masseur or masseuse to get blocked emotions flowing freely. Touch can be instrumental in opening up the pathways to emotion and help to release the anguish of grief. When we are trying to hold back painful emotions, we clench our muscles, locking in memories and thoughts that we have difficulty in dealing with.

Another effective method to facilitate forgiving and forgetting those who have hurt us is to write a letter to them, going into as much detail and depth as you can because this helps you to assuage the pain, to get it out of your system and to sleep better. There is no need to post the letter unless you feel this would be constructive because the positive aspect of the exercise is all in the writing.

Make decisions

Decide what, if anything, of a practical nature can be done to put things right and, if possible do it immediately or at the very first opportunity. If this works, go straight to step 6; if not, progress to the next step.

Reframe the problem

Reframe the problem area. Reframing is a strategy that stress managers use to find a positive benefit in an otherwise negative situation. By strategically choosing to view a problem as an opportunity, you automatically gain some leverage over it and this helps to reduce your feelings of distress and anxiety, raising morale and providing the momentum for change. The best way to illustrate this graphically is to visit an art shop. Take a picture and hold a variety of frames around it. See how different the picture looks with each frame? Even the overall mood of the picture can be influenced by the choice of frame.

Similarly, it is by encouraging the person with the problem to alter their frame of reference that positive benefits can be derived from negative situations. The man who was abused as a boy by his father can resolve that history will not repeat itself and reframe his outlook from victim to future role model as a father. The woman who was dumped by a boyfriend can reframe her outlook, see that he wasn't right for her and be motivated to find the partner who is.

Focus on the future

Focus on the future, not the past. The human mind is a vast reservoir of available resources. Nevertheless, it can only effectively focus on one thing at a time. When anger and guilt consume us, future prospects are completely out of mind and out of reach, but the morning after we forgive new avenues of opportunity open up if you let them. This is because, by then, you will have worked out the anger and guilt from your emotional system and, overnight, your mind will balance and adapt to this resolution.

Don't wallow in misery

Sacrifice your misery so that you don't wallow in it any longer. It is important that you are clear right from the outset about what it is that you will or won't be sacrificing. You'll been relinquishing nothing more valuable than your anguish and suffering. When you let go of that, your negative emotions and the heartache attached to them will be gone forever and you will feel lighter, better, so much more at peace with yourself. Naturally, you won't be sacrificing yourself or your ideals in any way, shape or form. Letting go of your misery and all of the painful emotions associated with it is the precursor to the act of forgiveness.

Be forgiving

Forgive yourself and everyone else. This can be a tough one and to some people it may seem like a completely alien concept. The act of forgiving must be a conscious choice because there can be no going back. It is most important that you complete the process of forgiving yourself and others. This can be difficult: the next chapter will show you how.

 The Bottom Line

Don't let your happiness be eroded by anger, resentment, guilt and regret; release the venom.

The power of forgiveness

If we could read the secret history of our enemies,
We would find in each man's life sorrow and
suffering enough to disarm hostility.

Henry Wadsworth Longfellow 1807–82

In this chapter, we are going to wipe the slate clean and move on. I know from my own life experiences and those of my clients that the exercise that follows will test you. The only way to heal the pain that will not let go is to forgive the person who hurt you and to forgive yourself at the same time for any complicity, omission or personal responsibility in the matter.

Forgiving erases the intensity of the hurt from your memory and allows you to move on. When you release the wrongdoer from the wrong, it's as if you're cutting a malignant tumour out from your inner self. You set a prisoner free, but you discover that the real prisoner was you. In demonstrating, that forgiveness can positively enhance emotional health, Professor Carl Thoresen of Stanford University, lead researcher for the Stanford Forgiveness Project, said, 'Very few people understand what forgiveness is and how it works.'

What is forgiveness?

Forgiveness is the act of cancelling an emotional debt from the wrongdoer to you and from you to yourself as well. It involves sacrificing your misery, along with the negative emotions and the heartache attached to them, in order to bring about a total transformation of feelings from anger, guilt, bitterness and resentment (even hate), to the healing state of understanding and acceptance.

What if I am not yet ready to forgive?

If you are still reading, then clearly you have reached the stage whereby you are at least prepared to contemplate forgiveness even if you do not feel you are ready or able to forgive just yet. Already you have come a very long way along the path towards forgiveness. I cannot believe that you will persist in torturing yourself forever now that relief from all that pain is within your grasp. Forgiving is a process that has a very definite start to it and you may be closer to the starting line than you thought possible days – even hours – ago. The start is deciding that in the end you will remove all blocks from your ideal of finding the right partner and enjoying a lasting relationship. To achieve that, you will forgive, you will recover from any setbacks; you will have the relationship you deserve.

Positive affirmation

This exercise is best done last thing at night, before you go to sleep. Sit down, stand to attention or kneel, whichever seems appropriate to you. Close your eyes and say these words aloud: 'The person I am going to forgive is... (name) and I forgive them for... (state briefly, in as few words as possible, what they did or said to hurt you).' Then say, 'I forgive myself for... (reason).' Repeat this three times, each time with increased emphasis, conviction and absolution in your voice and in your heart. Now we can really move on to enliven the future. Incidentally, many people tell me, and I experienced this myself, that you may well feel an innate sense of inner peace and calm when you wake up in the morning. This is because you have done the right thing, you have moved on to the healing phase of understanding and acceptance.

If you find this exercise in forgiveness is not appropriate for you at the moment, try dismissal. Whenever he/she comes back into your thoughts, bin 'em! This will achieve one of the primary benefits of forgiveness – closure: the end of the matter. Full stop. Dismissal is some way short of absolute forgiveness but it is a major step in the right direction.

 The Bottom Line

> Forgiveness allows you to move on to a new phase, one of understanding and acceptance.

CHAPTER 6

PART
3

Children

*Children begin by loving their parents; after a time, they
judge them; rarely, if ever, do they forgive them.*

Oscar Wilde 1854–1900

Life is a balancing act with myriad responsibilities but every one of
us owes it to ourselves to get a life. A good one! Our kids, pets and
ageing parents deserve the love and care we give them, but we
would be failing in our duty of care if we didn't put ourselves first
sometimes. Kids grow up, leave home, parents grow old and pass
away; so do pets. Where does that leave you if, in your desire to be
everything to everyone, you neglected yourself?

You merit a balanced, meaningful and joyful existence. You
won't get one unless you let love into your life. Don't allow
children or anyone else to override your responsibility to make
your life enjoyable.

But will anyone want me? The kids don't take kindly to visitors,
my mother can't be left alone for long periods and the German
Shepherd bites anyone who tries to take me into their arms.

It takes compassion, a sense of duty and patience to care for
others. These qualities are special and can help to fuel your love life
providing that you take the time and trouble to establish one.

Make a move in the direction of romance now! Don't wait for a more convenient time, when your life is all neatly in order. That day may be in a long time coming, and when it does the horizon may be bleak unless you seek to colour it while you have the opportunity.

No family relationship can ever be the same after a split, but there are some positive aspects for children in gaining stepparents and half-brothers and sisters. It can speed emotional maturity and interpersonal skills and in a best case scenario it can result in four interested adults being involved in their upbringing, rather than the traditional two, or the ever more frequent one.

Irishman Sir Bob Geldof, Boomtown Rats rocker turned Third World campaigner who won custody of his three daughters after a bitter legal battle, as well as becoming guardian of his former wife's daughter, passionately believes that 'two-parent families produce healthier, better-educated children'. Academia would appear to support his argument because new research published in October 2004 by Professor Charles Fesgorges of Exeter University demonstrates that children who are given additional educational support at home by parents (step or real) achieve up to 25 per cent better exam results than other children do. Tradition has it that children loathe their wicked stepmother or stepfather, but in many cases this just isn't true.

Many couples who successfully bring children from previous relationships into their new relationship take two very important steps. To begin with they make sure that the first few meetings with the children take place in a location that is fun and interesting for them, like a local amusement park, McDonald's, or Burger King. It's best to take children to places where they can't help but enjoy themselves. During these early meetings, the parent should carry on almost as if their new partner wasn't there. The new partner should appreciate but not intrude on the children's fun. If the newcomer comes on too strong too early, it can have the effect of alienating the children, and then the trouble really starts!

A mistake that many well-meaning newcomers make is to come across as too loving or too eager to please. This appears false and is most off-putting to children. Ideally, during these initial meetings, there shouldn't be any pressure on the children to interact with their parent's new partner. This is the 'let them get used to the intruder' stage – nothing more.

After several outings in which the children have experienced limited interaction with their mother's or father's new partner, it's time to progress to the next step whereby the children get accustomed to having this non-threatening adult in their lives. Let's say, for example, the new man in your life has sole custody of his two kids and he's in the habit of buying pizza and ice-cream and watching a movie with them at home on Friday nights. That's exactly what should continue to happen, the only difference being that you're there, too, sitting alongside him. Watch the movie and enjoy yourself, but don't get too affectionate. Afterwards, everyone helps to clear away the dishes if that's what normally happens and you make sure that you're part of the action as well.

The idea is to keep the kid's normal routine as intact as possible in the early weeks and months, that way you appear much less of a threat. Once they can feel confident that you are not going to upset their lives, that things will go on much as before, they will begin to relax and be more comfortable with you around.

The same principles apply if you're a man and the new woman in your life has children. If both of you have children, it's crucial that you take the trouble to choose a venue for the early meetings that all the kids will enjoy, not just some of them. If only one child is involved, it can be a good idea to let that child bring a friend. The first time I introduced my teenage daughter Danielle to Tatiana, I invited Danielle to choose the venue for lunch and told her that she was welcome to bring a friend with her, if she wanted to. In the event, she chose a pizza house and brought her best friend along with her, easing the pressure on all of us. Slow and steady is the key.

Let's share a little bluntness. Children can be difficult and downright awkward when a new person comes into your life. Not everybody finds it easy to discipline their children, especially in a new and emotionally threatening situation. If you are one of these parents – and there are hundreds of thousands of us – you have to find a way to make your children understand that your happiness is important as well as theirs.

If your children are liable to brush off anything you say that doesn't please them, you need to confront them. As soon as they ignore you, pull them up short and insist that they listen to you. You won't find this easy, but if you persist in demanding their respect – it is your right to be respected – you will find a huge improvement in their behaviour. Only when they treat you properly will they be able to think about treating your partner as you would want him/her to be treated.

Convince them that you love them every bit as much now – with a new partner in your life – as you did when it was just you and them together. Stick at it and you will succeed in alleviating their fears that they are being pushed out, cheated or sidelined in what might have seemed like competition for your love.

Does this seem terrifying? That's because it is. But don't forget that no matter how great the challenge, it's one-step-at-a-time stuff and if you persevere, you will have every chance of achieving the stable relationship you seek.

 The Bottom Line

Honour your responsibilities, but stand up and make a life for yourself.

Personal safety: taking the initiative

Great emergencies and crises show us how much greater our vital resources are than we had supposed.

William James 1842–1910

Before we get actively involved in the dating scene – as we will in Part 4 – bearing in mind that some readers may have been out of circulation for a while, let's dust off a few elementary precautions, some of which apply equally to men and women, others predominantly to women. The information here will not sound the slightest bit romantic, but it might save your life or at least get you out of a tight spot. Some of the more basic points are:

1 Elementary precautions when dating

2 AIDS/HIV awareness

3 Dealing with pick-up artists, sirens and serial charmers

4 Drink-spikers and drug-rapists

5 Exit strategy.

Elementary precautions when dating

When you're out with your friends and you're on the lookout for someone new, be flexible and separate when you arrive at your chosen venue if the mood takes you, but arrange beforehand to get back together towards the end of the evening. If you come together, you leave together, unless you agree that it is perfectly safe to do otherwise. If you meet someone promising and the feeling is mutual, they'll be prepared to arrange to meet you another time, when you've both had the opportunity to find out a little more about each other. The next meeting should also take place in a public place like a bar or restaurant, or somewhere where you feel relaxed and safe and other people are around.

If you have arranged to meet someone by using a dating service, online, through a personal ad in a newspaper or magazine (even the quality press), don't assume that you already know him or her just because you have spoken on the telephone or in a chat room. For safety's sake, meet only in public places initially, tell a friend where you're going and who you will be meeting, take your cell phone and arrange your own transportation home.

AIDS/HIV awareness

This book is for people seeking lasting love, not sexual athletes. But the rise in AIDS/HIV/sexually transmitted diseases means that anyone who intends to have sex should not only take sensible precautions to protect themselves from the risk of exposure, but they should also decide a personal code of conduct in these matters now, if they haven't already done so. The risk of AIDS/HIV is yet another reason why making love within the safe and secure confines of a mutually faithful and permanent relationship is the desire of an ever increasing number of people in this enlightened age.

Each of us must make a decision about how to conduct our social lives in the wake of the AIDS/HIV nightmare. It seems to me that there are five rational choices:

- Total abstinence except within the security of a faithful and permanent relationship.

- Engaging in 'safe sex' (intercourse with condoms and contraceptive jelly or cream). The words 'safe sex' should be taken with a pinch of salt. The wretched rubber things have been known to split open at some stage during intercourse and, in any event, they're not 100 per cent safe. They are, however, much safer than sex without condoms.

- Restricting the range of sexual activity. There's a lot you can do without exchanging bodily fluids!

- Trusting your instinct and judgement in your choice of sexual partners.

- Getting yourself tested for HIV and insisting on negative test results from anyone with whom you plan to have sex with in the future. Many couples about to embark on a permanent relationship do this.

What is your personal policy on sex? Will it stand up to a reality check after a romantic dinner for two or a damn good night clubbing with someone really good looking and sexy when the beat of the music, the throb of sensual excitement, the raw pang of lust makes you all steamed up and ready for sex? Would you be able to resist the overwhelming psychological compulsion that makes some of us take chances in a parked car, in the back porch or in bed?

Dealing with pick-up artists, sirens and serial charmers
Pick-up artists – both the male and female variety – are invariably charming and consummate manipulators. They should be, they've had lots of practice at it with people like you. Usually, they just want to seduce you, use you or play with your heart for the sheer exhilaration and hell of it, but things can get worse. If you're

particularly unlucky, they'll make off with your money, your possessions and your reputation as well! They mask their intentions by creating a mood of comfort and pleasure so that you feel so much better about yourself. They give you the impression that they understand your problems and feel your pain, adapting effortlessly to your moods and body language.

Their method is simple: the male variety – the rake or the charmer – tends to deflect attention from themselves and focus all their attention on you; and the female of the species – the siren – captivates men with her appearance, her manner and her availability. She listens intently to you as you tell her all about yourself and your desires. You will discover, too late, that you know little about her because you have been talking about you. As Benjamin Disraeli said, 'Talk to a man about himself and he will listen for hours.' The same applies to women.

No man can resist having his ego massaged and every woman enjoys being charmed by a genuine admirer, but if your pick-up appears to have an immediate connection with you and seems too good to be true, he or she probably is! Beware of the person who is so relaxed and generous with their compliments that you feel you want to tell them everything about you, particularly if they scan the room from time to time while talking to you. Don't accept drinks or favours from would-be seducers like this or offer them anything at all yourself unless you are willing to fall prey to their illusionist charms.

Many otherwise intelligent men and women overstate their ability to handle just such a situation. A couple of extra drinks can tilt the balance of control away from you, rendering you vulnerable. Keep all personal information to yourself and make it very clear that you are not interested. Be direct and blunt if necessary, turning or walking away if all else fails. If you allow yourself to be taken in, enchanted and disarmed by their magic, don't be surprised when your heart is left dangling like a puppet on a string while they give someone else the treatment a few days, weeks, months, or years down the line.

Drink-spikers and drug-rapists
This is a fast-growing crime in the USA, the UK and throughout Europe and although people who spike drinks by slipping substances like Rohypnol or GHB into them are usually men in gangs of three or four, women are believed to do it too. According to Professor Betsy Stanko, a criminologist, *'The typical profile of a gang drug-rapist is a man who displays normal behaviour, has no criminal record and is either a professional or from a privileged background. Gang drug-rape is seen as a sport that goes unchallenged, which is why they continue to get away with it. Because these men are often charming, good-looking, well-educated and successful, there is an element of "I can have whatever I want".'*

The effect of even a minute quantity of one of these drugs can be to render the recipient disorientated, confused and easy to manipulate off the premises and into bed. Within a short period, the person targeted will be in a dreamlike state, drifting in and out of consciousness, unclear about what has or hasn't happened. To avoid any possibility of this happening to you, never leave your drink unattended or, if you do, when you return, discard it and buy a new one. Alternatively, use a product called *Drink Detector,* available from leading chemists and pharmacies.

Exit strategy
If you are under threat – spiking, drug-rape, or whatever – just go! Accept no courtesies or offers to drive you home. Get a taxi and go. Many victims of rape or violence have reported that they had a feeling something bad was going to happen, but were too embarrassed or self-conscious to act on their feelings. They say it's like a sixth sense, a warning bell in your head. Should you experience this sensation, act on it and exit immediately.

If your date turns out to be a mistake – as often happens with blind dates – married, too old, too young, too *other*, more delicacy is required. For me, the direct but sympathetic approach is best. 'This is not going to work out for me. Let's finish our drinks and say goodbye.' But I must caution you about being too hasty in your judgement because I know of some great relationships that got off to a pretty shaky start.

Some people fabricate exit strategies to terminate blind dates by going off to the restroom and using their mobile to phone a friend, asking them to ring back in a few minutes when they're back with their date, feigning an emergency at home or at work. 'My uncle's dropped down dead!' or 'I'm an auxiliary fireman and my station needs me!' If that is your preferred way of wimping out, fine, but I suggest this simply prolongs the awkwardness, the embarrassment and the hurt to the other party.

We've taken a precautionary trawl through the darker side of dating. The chances are that – other than the occasional disappointing date – none of these scenarios will happen to you. Do not let this chapter put you off going for gold in your quest for the ideal mate. It merely serves to remind you of the hazards of dating and to illustrate, by contrast, one of the major plusses of a secure and lasting relationship: trust in your partner.

The Bottom Line

Be aware of the risks, take sensible precautions and live your life to the absolute maximum.

Freedom to start again

Whatever you can do, or dream you can, begin it.
Boldness has genius, power and magic in it.

Goethe 1749–1832, from John Anster's translation of *Faust*

This is your life and you are free to start again. Seize the initiative and vow never to give up the search for Mr or Ms Absolutely Right until you are physically enjoying the relationship of your life. Remember that wishing, hoping and regretting are the most common and dangerous tactics for evading the action you need to take to kick-start your love life. In the remaining pages of this book, you will find the tools you need to go for gold in the relationships market. Don't sell yourself short, don't settle for second best and certainly don't live alone unless you want to, because no matter how glossy a picture they paint in magazines, life is a desert without love.

As you look back on your life, you'll find it's not so much the things that you did that torment you, but the things that you could have done and didn't. Two of the saddest words in the English language are *'If only'*.

Six letters between them and yet they have the power to immobilise strong hunky men and highly eligible women and render them redundant at any age in the world of relationships. These words crop up repeatedly whenever new clients arrive for stress management. *'If only* it wasn't for... my mother, the kids, my job, the state of my finances, my weight, my age, my ex, my depression, the place where I live, etc, etc.'

The trouble with *'if only'* is that it doesn't change anything. It keeps you stuck in your present situation facing the wrong way – backwards to the past instead of forwards to the future. Far better to change *'if only'* for the words *'this time...'*

It pays to prepare for love and to command the interpersonal skills and the expertise to manage a relationship constructively, but we shouldn't put our love life on hold until everything is in place. It can be a mistake to put your search for love on the back burner until you accomplish certain goals because life does not divide easily into convenient little compartments. Love can be very elusive if you close yourself off – either intentionally or subconsciously – to the possibility of love. It cannot be relied upon to show up just when it suits you!

A surprising number of high-achievers assume that they must put their lives neatly in order before they can enter a meaningful relationship, but it is just as logical and far more realistic to take the view that meeting the right person will help you to make the best of yourself; and you'll be having much more fun while you're at it! As long as you have genuine motives for wanting a relationship, it is not necessary to have the practical elements of your life – career, house, car, finances, physical fitness, optimum weight, etc – in order before you open your heart to someone really special. Having your life perfectly together offers many advantages but may appear intimidating, even boring, to others.

Whether or not you win in love has little to do with the availability of eligible people within your neighbourhood, place of work or circle of friends and everything to do with your sense of purpose and your determination to find precisely the right partner. If we believe in something, and if we want it enough, we can do quite amazing things – even greater than we dare to imagine.

The Bottom Line

Freedom to start again is saying, '*This time I will,*' instead of '*If only...*'

PART 4

Contact

*I figure that the degree of difficulty
in combining two lives ranks somewhere
between re-routing a hurricane and
finding a parking place in
downtown Manhattan.*

Claire Cloninger

CHAPTER 1

PART
4

The search for Mr or Ms Absolutely Right

Nothing extraordinary, great or beautiful is ever accomplished without thinking about it more often and better than others.

King Louis XIV of France 1643–1715

Let's get serious about searching for Mr or Ms Absolutely Right. To start with, we need to find out more about your ideal partner and then it will be necessary to gently probe your lifestyle to see what changes, if any, you should make in order to leap, lurch or launch yourself on to the dating scene. We need to do some sober thinking in order to take strategic action, so ask yourself three simple but vital questions:

1 Who am I looking for?

2 Why?

3 Where am I going to find this person?

The answers to questions 1 and 2 might seem blatantly obvious to you, but we are leaving nothing to chance. You need to know what you want before you can be sure of getting it. You also need to be able to recognise it when it's staring you in the face. Otherwise, you could find yourself missing opportunity after opportunity, or, even worse – when the intoxication of love clears sufficiently for you to see what you have done – you might be with someone who is no good for you and you will be responsible for the mess, as you didn't do the necessary groundwork in a crucial area of your life.

So that you do not suffer this terrible fate (the divorced, jilted and trapped will know that I do not exaggerate), I want you to list, in order of importance, five qualities that you rate highly in a potential partner. If you normally just go out on spec, trusting in fate to deliver your perfect partner, now is the time to wise-up unless you're looking for a one-nighter or a dead-end romance, in which case you're reading the wrong book!

Do not take more than 60 seconds to complete this task. When your list is complete, remind yourself exactly why it is you are looking for someone to love. You can take as long as you like over that one.

The five most important qualities that I shall look for when dating are:

1 . . . .

2 . . . .

3 . . . .

4 . . . .

5 . . . .

Why do I want someone to love and someone to love me in a permanent relationship?

1 . . . .

2 . . . .

3 . . . .

4 . . . .

5 . . . .

6 . . . .

There is no right or wrong list of qualities or reasons to love because we are unique and different individuals. The sole purpose of this exercise has been to concentrate your mind on your priorities.

Now that you have answered two of the three questions at the start of this chapter: *Who am I looking for,* and *Why?* the time has come to address the final question: *Where am I going to find this person?* The choices are laid out for you across two chapters – this one and the next – but first, let's get a grip on the relative ease or complexity of the task at hand. Then it will be up to you to decide whether you want to do things the Countdown way or make hard work of it.

In nature, the process of finding a mate is relatively straightforward. Creatures large and small indicate their readiness by fanning their plumage, howling or tweeting in a certain way, or, in the case of one particular species, by changing the colour of their buttocks. Potential suitors present themselves, then vie for the right to mate. It all progresses swimmingly and there is very little opportunity to mess up, get embarrassed or suffer the complexities of a broken heart.

Among humans, however, finding the ideal mate has more in common with winning the lottery than the laws of nature; the odds of scooping the jackpot are daunting, and disappointment is widespread. From the initial attraction of setting eyes upon someone who invades the crevices of your mind and your soul, to the hazards of approaching, meeting, dating, falling in love with, undressing and sleeping with that individual, you are taking your heart in your hands at every stage.

With human nature so much less predictable than Mother Nature and the improbability of the two of you being just right for each other mentally, physically and emotionally, you need a reliable means to test the long-term viability of your proposed relationship.

When the time comes and you have found the person you believe is the one, you will, for the first time, be in a position to stack the odds in your favour and measure the value of your relationship against The Matchmaking Equation, a powerful tool that's coming soon. This will give you the confidence to know, before you get in too deep, whether or not your proposed relationship has the capacity to develop and become permanent.

In dating, perhaps more than in any other aspect of life, you've got to be in a position to know when to quit and move on, and how to cope when things don't work out as you would have wished. If you're reckless or you panic, if you say or do the wrong thing, or do the right thing but at the wrong time, the consequences can be irreversible, emotionally damaging, life threatening or life producing. That's why we are going to proceed progressively through the dating process in this part of the book.

If you haven't dated for 10, 20, 30 years, or if you went out last night on a date and made a real hash of things, or if you did everything right but it just didn't work out, don't worry, we'll get things sorted, and we will keep on going until you do meet Mr or Ms Absolutely Right. We won't quit until you are happy, together and destined to become a magnificent twosome – with the sole proviso being that you are determined to succeed.

Even in this age of off-planet tourist travel (Thank you, Virgin!), most people find their partner within five miles of their own front door, their local supermarket or their place of work. When it comes to potential partners, the streets really are paved with gold. But do you know how to prospect for this human gold?

You know how you spend your time. Does it bring you in contact with new people in the right bracket? If you stay at home a lot, cooking, cleaning, watching telly, looking after children, working from home, etc, do you make time for meeting new people? Probably not. So, you're going to have to make changes!

Perhaps you do meet new people but you still haven't met the right person. Does this not suggest that changes have to be made, this time focusing on *you?*

Let's look at your lifestyle and see how many different ways you can find to work a new strategy into your day-to-day routine. I'll give you a few examples of how other people have turned the pavements to gold by introducing date-yielding changes to their general way of doing things and then you decide what variations in routine will be comfortable for you.

Bit by bit, as you fit these new arrangements into your everyday life, you should find that life becomes more interesting and that you are meeting more eligible people. Now that you know the sort of qualities you are looking for in a potential partner, it will be so much easier to recognise someone who embodies those special qualities when you meet them. Keep on with this strategy, adjusting your approach from time to time, if you feel the need.

What about using your shopping time? In addition to doing your usual shopping routine, take in some stores where your kind of partner is likely to be. Mind you, this can be tricky so be prepared to experiment. Few of us get it right first time!

On the way home, where, naturally, if it's a man you're after, you will have taken a good look in the men's clothing department of your local department store, you might want to call by a couple of health clubs to check out the man factor. You don't have to join, or even exercise, just tell the club's receptionist that you want to see the facilities on offer and ask for a free conducted tour. If your type of men is pumping iron all over the place, it might be in your interest to join. Ice-skating and rollerblading rinks are well worth a try, too. Men just love to help beginners like you.

If you are bored one Saturday afternoon, you might want to team up with a girlfriend and try your luck at a football, rugby or polo match. Don't be put off by TV portrayal of football hooliganism; there's lots of congenial socialising that goes on before and after the whistle, and at half time! There will be no shortage of single men of all ages there, most of them, decent blokes, and, as a spectator, it doesn't matter how little you know about the sport. Just say, when you get chatting, you fancied doing something different for a change!

On the assumption that you are a single, straight guy going out for your solo-shop, think where your ideal woman is likely to be and take in the cosmetic counters and the women's clothing departments. No need to be embarrassed, you could be considering a birthday present for your sister! But you will not be asked to explain.

If you normally have your hair cut at a barber's shop, change to a unisex salon, and don't rule out the occasional visit to an alternative health centre for an Indian head massage or an aromatherapy session. Bookshops, music stores, art galleries and exhibitions are great places for both sexes to check out because people seem to linger for longer and there are many opportunities to ask questions and get talking.

We have been concentrating on the customers or users of these places. Don't forget the staff! A fair percentage of them will be standing there wishing and hoping that Mr or Ms Absolutely Right would walk into their life.

Open days and trial sessions for adult education classes is fertile territory for meeting positively minded people of the opposite sex, or the same sex, if you are that way inclined, because you are all in the same boat, you're all on a learning curve. There is much to talk about. Don't just consider courses that naturally interest you, think also about which classes your ideal partner might find interesting! Cooking classes can be a good bet because you sometimes get lots of single and divorced men and women on courses like these.

If you have school-age kids, school fund-raising events yield more than money; they generate single parents, male and female, by the carload. If your kids left school years ago, how about computer-programming, drama, writing or painting classes?

No matter what age you are, events like the London Marathon, Henley Regatta, Notting Hill Carnival, Glastonbury and the Motor Show and venues such as the Eden Project generate tens of thousands of interesting people, many of them single, who are intent on enjoying life. I have mentioned only a few such events in the south-east and south-west of England, but there are many more all over the country and in countries throughout the world. The important message here is get outside, mingle, engage others in conversation and get yourself a date with someone fabulous. Generally, people at events like this are feeling happy, excited and in the right frame of mind to be friendly towards you.

Feeling brave? What do you really enjoy doing? Is it something that others could be interested in learning more about? You may be the very person your local adult education college is looking for. Approach them! Who knows, Mr or Ms Absolutely Right might be the first person to walk straight in through the classroom door. One thing that is for sure: if you meet your prospective partner this way, you will share at least one keen interest right away.

Do you live in a rural area? Use the local village hall to start a social club for single people. Put up notices in surrounding villages. As the host, you're in a position to talk to everyone that comes. Just imagine how much this will help your chances of dating to spiral up!

Saturday nights! What do you normally do? Stay in and watch TV, dial out for a takeaway, or go round to a friend's house for a drink and a chat? If so, why not link up with someone more outgoing and have Saturday night out on the town? A quick look in your local paper's 'What's on' guide will give you options galore.

Some of the established wine clubs have wine-tasting sessions over the weekend, or you could join a singles club. Many of them cater for all age groups and they organise many different events, some of which may appeal to you. Let your friends know that you're doing things the Countdown way from now on and you would appreciate it if they invited you to parties and events where other singles will be there, too.

Many people meet their partners through work. If you work for a medium or large organisation, make a point of going to social get-togethers even if you found previous occasions to be something of a non-event. You only have to be lucky once.

Business or employee training courses can be another source of meeting new people, where there is often a natural feeling of camaraderie among the delegates. Find out about courses that would be beneficial to your employer for you to attend – no matter how small an employer you work for – and suggest they book you on the course at the firm's expense.

Not exciting enough for you? Well, how about the occasional night out at a casino? You don't need to spend more than a tenner having a flutter on the slot machines and I would advise you not to gamble unless you know what you're doing and you can afford to do it. But these days it's not all gangsters, rogues and compulsive gamblers. Decent people go there too, and many of them are single!

No money to flutter? Okay, but here's a time-proven method that gets results time after time, no matter where you live – and you are paid, too! Work two or three shifts a week in a pub or a wine bar. Twenty-five years ago my sister's first husband walked out on her, leaving her devastated and broke, with two very young kids to look after. Although she was accustomed to working in a bank, she took a part-time job in a pub and within a few short months she met the man that was to be her future husband and they continue to be very happily married to this day.

My first wife Valerie, although we lived in north London when we split up, decided to go into central London to expand her range of social contacts. She worked for a short time in a pub close to New Scotland Yard. It wasn't long before she met a sparky and loving detective who swept her off her feet and they too have been happily married ever since.

To sum up, you have a lot more chance of pulling across the bar than in it, but don't make the mistake of working in your local pub. The idea is to meet new people, not the same old crowd!

What do you usually do on Sundays? Do you have your newspaper delivered and read it leisurely at home? Cancel it! Take a stroll or a drive to your nearest newsagent and buy it, then relax and enjoy reading it in public, on a park bench, in a wine bar or at a place that serves good coffee. Choose a seat where you're easily visible; there's life out there and there is someone who really wants to meet you. Perhaps this person is a friend of a friend?

The very next time you see someone you like the look of but you don't know personally, at a friend's party, in a neighbour's garden, chatting to someone you know in your local supermarket, take a deep breath and summon up the courage to introduce yourself. If you don't feel able to do that, that's okay but don't be coy about asking your friend or neighbour if they're single. If so, drop some hints that you would very much appreciate an introduction.

Let's get some high-octane action going here! Friends can turn out to be an absolute goldmine when it comes to putting one and one together at a dinner party, and sparking a date that fits! But, usually, they must be asked. Most friends don't go willingly into matchmaking mode without plenty of encouragement and a few gentle reminders from you. Who do you know that might enjoy acting as Cupid for you? Make a list now of people who could help you and add more names to the list as they come to mind, as they will do, over the course of the next few days.

When you're in the mood (a glass of wine or a stiff gin and tonic generally helps), give each of them a ring. Don't sound like a wimp, or a robotic beggar on a mission from some American dating programme; say something like, 'Hi, I'm bored! Any chance you're free this evening/next week for a mad night out? Got any interesting single mates?' If this suggestion fills you with trepidation, remind yourself that more people meet their partners through a friend or a friend of a friend than any other method of introduction currently available.

The Bottom Line

Change your existing routine so that you have a better chance to date. Take the initiative now.

CHAPTER 2

PART
4

Virtual, media and professional options

Words may be false and full of art;
sighs are the natural language of the heart.

Thomas Shadwell 1642–92

'Where are all the single men?' 'Where are all the single women?' 'Where are all the gay and lesbian people?'

'Right here, only a credit card transaction away,' is the deafening response from the internet service providers, the personal ads section of virtually every newspaper in the land, the speed-dating and dating industries, and the introduction agencies and marriage bureaux. But can we believe them? Yes and no is the answer because it's very hit-and-miss. Millions of people do meet this way. Millions more are disappointed. I'll lay out the options, you decide what's right for you.

The virtual world of internet dating

Some people, mainly traditionalists, take the view that internet dating is the last resort for the sad and desperate, but this is not an enlightened response to an industry that has seen online personal ads in the UK alone rise from half a million to 3.5 million between 2003 and 2005. A good friend of mine, after many years of living alone following the death of his wife from cancer, decided to try his luck on the internet, and the result: a beautiful Canadian woman called Jo-Anne who was tempted across the Atlantic to meet him. They have been happily married and living in Polperro for many years now, and this year life becomes even more exciting for them – they are selling their business in the village and relocating to Canada.

Success can never be guaranteed in this cyber world of vast potential, but online dating is now generally regarded as sociably acceptable, widespread and used by men and women across the age span. Darren Richards, the creator of Britain's largest online dating service, DatingDirect.com, now has 1.5 million active members. Since 1999, the company has chalked up dozens of marriages of people who met via the website. The basic rules of dating online are:

- Select the right site for you – there are lots to choose from. Decide first if you simply want to post your profile on the internet at nominal or no cost, or if you want to sign up with an online dating agency, which will involve completing a personal questionnaire and paying a regular monthly fee.

- When you post your profile on the internet, make it interesting, eye-catching and direct. Experienced cyberspace users surf through profiles quickly. You must create an intriguing first impression or you won't hold their attention for more than half-a-second.

- Include a photo profile and you will receive up to eight times more responses.

- If you receive lewd or disgusting e-mails, report them direct to the site administrator.

- When you make contact with someone who seems promising, get in touch with him or her straight away, making sure that your message is brief, entertaining and relevant.

- Talk on the telephone, as well as exchanging e-mails. You can tell a lot about someone from their voice and their telephone manner. Understand that you are not in a safeguarded or supportive environment.

- Don't feel pressured into revealing more about you than you want to, and bear in mind that people exaggerate, use photos that are 15 years out of date and tell porkies like there's no tomorrow on the internet.

- Learn to take no for an answer, because when someone doesn't reply it's because they're not interested.

- When you arrange to meet someone for the first time, for safety's sake meet in a public place like a bar or restaurant, take your mobile phone with you and make sure someone knows where you are and when you expect to be home. Call them when you get back, to confirm.

Personal ads in the media

Newspapers and magazines in the west have traditionally provided facilities for lonely hearts to place lineage advertisements in the personal columns of their publications, complete with a box number to which respondents could reply by letter. The upfront cost of these advertisements varies depending on the circulation and popularity of the publication.

Advertisements today are generally placed 'free' by calling premium-rate telephone numbers. You record a short profile for publication in the personal columns and on the publisher's website, to which a box number or a voice number is allocated. Callers reply to individual advertisements or collect their messages by telephoning another premium rate line. Some papers even display the advertiser's photo online to give browsers a combined audio, visual and literate experience.

Despite the growing popularity of internet dating, the personal pages of newspapers and magazines are still hugely popular and they get results – not all the time, but some of the time. Many of the rules that apply to internet dating are equally relevant here, but targeting and choice of publication is an area where many people go wrong.

For instance, if you are a Cornish pig farmer with an award-winning piggery in the middle of nowhere and you want a wife who will be happy living down on the farm, *Farmers Weekly* or *Country Life* is the place for you. Or is it? How can you be sure that the prospect of love on the farm won't appeal to a *Daily Mail* or a *Sunday Times* reader? Or a woman from a nearby village whose first point of reference is her local paper? If you're going this route, choose at least one appropriately targeted publication, a local paper and a national big-hitter as well.

Professional options

If I had to slice and pigeonhole this part of the industry into just three divisions, I would do it like this:

- Speed dating

- Get-together organisers

- Introduction agencies and marriage bureaux

Speed dating is a growing phenomenon that originated in the USA and is now well established on the UK dating scene. It's fast-moving and fun to do and the biggest thing it has going for it is that you can tell at once if there is any chemistry between you and your five-minute partner. There is no time to get bored because any self-respecting organiser will line up lots of brief encounters in one exhausting session, and in the event that two of you reckon you want to get together for longer, the occasion will at least have resulted in a firm date.

Get together organisers include big names like 'Only Lunch' and 'Dinner Dates' and a host of similar organisations around the country. Many of them, despite their seemingly restrictive names, organise all sorts of social events for meeting other single people, such as parties, balls, opera and theatre evenings, gallery visits and sports events. In common with all things in life, there's good and there's not so good. I always think that it's a good idea to ask if you can attend a trial event to see how you get on before paying to become a member.

Introduction agencies and marriage bureaux largely cover much the same ground except that top-of-the-range specialist agencies and bureaux carry out exacting and thorough vetting and matching services and charge anywhere between £3,500 and £15,000. Some bureaux have a special understanding and expertise with particular ethnic groups such as the Asian or Jewish community. Understandably, for that sort of money, you can expect to receive a high level of personalised service where only the database is computer driven.

There will always be a demand for introduction services from singletons who do not know how to go about finding themselves a suitable partner, and from executives in demanding jobs who are unable or unwilling to make time available to manage their personal affairs. But I can't help wondering – if these people genuinely can't afford the time to find the right partner – how on earth are they going to find the time to invest in the relationship to make it a loving and lasting one?

The bulk of the mass-market introduction services, which generally charge a few hundred pounds per member, rely almost entirely on computer-generated dates, although some agencies take the trouble to screen prospective members in person at the outset. Do satisfy yourself that the interviewer/salesperson has the professional experience to screen and assess you, or you could find yourself being processed into the system on a 'commission-on-sign-up' basis.

Think before going blindly into a system on the assumption that the computer always knows best. Check with any of your friends or work colleagues who have experienced a system based on computer-dating! In this cruelly commercial world, love and the selection of Mr or Ms Absolutely Right is one area of life where it pays enormous dividends to learn how to do it yourself.

Have you ever wished you could access an environment where virtually every single person you meet, is genuinely looking for a lasting relationship with the right partner? Where people have demonstrated their commitment to interpersonal development, by investing time and resources in finding out how meaningful relationships work?

Such an environment is being created right now by The Countdown Organisation at locations across the country. Each of these venues is a no-go area for anyone who is not sincere about wanting a committed and lasting relationship when they meet the right partner. Access is exclusive to Countdown readers, seminar delegates and workshop participants who have transformed unresourceful emotions into empowering actions.

The most striking and obvious benefit of looking for Mr or Ms Absolutely Right in a Countdown-cultivated environment is the absence of people who are not emotionally available, willing or ready to enter a meaningful relationship, along with those who are dating for spurious reasons. Great relationships take two active participants to create, the more equal, the better.

If finding possible and suitable partners is the bit that fazes you, we can help. The Countdown Organisation offers strategies that, to be frank, are superior to most in that they cut down the risk and are more likely to lead to the right person in the shortest time. There are contact details at the back of this book or you can visit www.countdowntolove.com.

The Bottom Line

You've read about the options on offer, but only you can decide what's right for you.

Relax – this is going to be easier than you think

Like a ship that's rounded the Cape, you will find yourself in calm water, the raging sea subsided, floating on gentle waves.

Marcus Aurelius BCE 121–80

Very soon you are going to start dating and you won't give up until you find the one. You will test the wisdom of that choice against the Matchmaking Equation before you get in too deep and you will take corrective action if necessary. You will fall in love with your ideal partner, I have no doubt, and you will build the foundations to a relationship that will be happy, rewarding and permanent. You will make it to magnificent twosomeness and don't let anyone tell you otherwise or knock you off course.

This is not just positive thinking going on in the forefront of your mind; this is your future. But now that you know for sure you're going ahead with the Countdown approach to romance, it's only natural for second thoughts to begin to creep in to the furthermost corners of your mind, just as sure as if someone had thrown cold water all over your plans. You begin to worry about how you will cope and you become anxious at the prospect of dating. Anxiety is the last thing you need when you go out on a date, so we are going to deal with it here in this chapter by preparing you properly for what is to come so that you have nothing to be anxious about.

Finding the right partner is a serious matter because it can greatly enhance the meaning and quality of your life and yet it is attained by simultaneously doing two things that might appear to be opposites. On the one hand, you need a definitive and workable plan – you have that in your hands – and you should put it effectively into action to be sure of succeeding. On the other, you must be relaxed, easy-going and anxiety-free so that your date finds you delightful to be with.

How are we going to deal with these opposing tensions? In two ways: by getting ready for what's to come and by smoothing away your fears, to enable you to be on top form for your date. When you are confident that you know what to do and how to do it, you create a frame of mind in which your worries tend to let go and drift away naturally, because you remove the anchor of self-doubt to which your doubts and anxieties cling.

By observing the simple guidelines that follow, you will be ready for virtually any dating situation and you too can be anxiety-free. Let's start by getting ourselves in the mood for a relaxed and enjoyable date so that the lucky person who will have the pleasure of your company is likely to find you irresistible. We've already dealt with the power of attraction in Part 2. Here we will concentrate on preparation, attitude and the basic essentials of date management.

Attitude
Fine-tune your attitude. To succeed in any long-term relationship you need to be co-operative, flexible, emotionally available, honest

and committed to making things work out for your mutual benefit. Start as you mean to carry on! You may not yet have any idea whether the person you are meeting has real relationship potential, but it is foolish to even contemplate a date unless you intend to approach it with a positive, upbeat attitude, focusing on the pleasing aspects of your date.

Venue

Have a say in choosing the place where you're going to meet. Popular choices are upmarket but unpretentious restaurants, wine bars, comedy clubs or jazz venues. Locations like these are favourites for first dates, because you'll enjoy a convivial atmosphere without having to try too hard. Comedy performances offer the added benefit of allowing you to see if your date has a sense of humour.

Timing

If you're the first to arrive, don't panic; someone has to get there first! Relax, order yourself a drink, positioning yourself, either at the bar or seated, so that you have a clear view of the entrance and can easily spot your date, welcoming him or her with a warm smile, regardless of your inner feelings about being kept waiting. Remember, the idea is to be irresistible!

Smile

Everyone becomes more attractive when they smile. Why is a smile so powerful? Because it communicates warmth and draws people towards you. People remember first impressions most strongly, so if you greet them with a warm smile, you get off to a cracking start in any social situation. Brian Bates, co-author of the BBC book and television series *The Human Face,* confirms the importance of smiling in society:

'We would often rather share our confidences, hopes and money with smilers for deep reasons which are often beyond our conscious

awareness. Spontaneous smilers have been shown to have a more successful life in personal and career terms.'

It is a fact that smiling takes much less effort than frowning, involves less muscular tension and is more spontaneous. The human body even rewards us for smiling! When we smile, the mere act of doing it boosts the production of endorphins in our brain, releasing natural energisers and painkillers throughout our body. This is why smiling creates a pleasant ambience, helps you to relax and puts your date at ease.

Breathe

Would it surprise you to hear that most people don't know how to breathe and talk at the same time? Your voice sounds far richer, more controlled and lovelier to listen to when you speak on the out breath, as you exhale, rather than when you breathe in.

As an experiment now, try talking to yourself as you breathe in. Within a few moments, your voice begins to sound strangled, doesn't it? Now take a deep breath, then talk to yourself as you exhale. Can you hear the difference? Not only is there more clarity and variety in your voice, the tone of your voice sounds more seductive and interesting. So many people on first dates are on the verge of fainting because anxiety, stiffness and shallow breathing conspire to make their conversation sound wooden. Breathe more deeply, talk on the out breath and the words that you say will sound nicer to the ear, and you will feel more relaxed and in control of your speech.

Speak

Speak with enthusiasm! Enthusiasm is contagious, it breeds excitement in others and it is the key to influencing people in a positive way. People tend to come alive and feel happier when they are in the company of someone who is enthusiastic. Such positive feelings contribute to the bonds of friendship that strengthen people's attachments to each other.

If you can't think what to say, ask a question! Questions are great icebreakers and it is easy to pick up on something that your date says in reply to propel the conversation forward.

One of the worst sins you can commit on a date is to be boring and one of the best things you can do is to get your date talking about themselves. This way you learn a lot more about them, you take the heat off yourself and you endear yourself to your date because of the genuine interest you are showing in them. Get your date talking about his or her hobbies, holidays, job, profession, aspirations, and when you hear something good or meaningful of which you approve, compliment them. Flattery is fine as long as it's genuine. It's a terrific way of making a memorable impression.

Listen

Listen with interest to what your date has to say. People, generally, when given the opportunity, love talking about themselves. As this is the first date, allow your companion to do most of the talking on any subject that interests them. You can easily draw them out of their shell by making them feel comfortable talking to you. An easy way to do this is by temporarily adopting the role of an interested student who is keen to learn more from someone who is clearly informed. Strategically, this will help you to secure their friendship and, when honed to perfection, it can set the scene for your date to fall effortlessly in love with you.

Body language

It is a fact that both men and women are infinitely more drawn to someone who appears to like them and clearly enjoys their company. During your first meeting, smile warmly whenever the occasion permits. Eye contact is vital at this moment. Don't stare. Just look into their eyes for longer than usual, look away, then glance back. Keep your arms open in a relaxed, inviting position and lean forward periodically, nodding agreement whenever you hear something with which you concur.

Develop interest in what is being said because your body language is revealing your true feelings, whether you like it or not. If you allow your shoulders to droop, the message staring your date in the face is: you're bored! If you cross your arms firmly, you're telling him or her you are on the defensive. Your attention should be on your companion's face, because if you are sincerely interested in hearing more, this is the first place your date will look for encouragement.

Laughter
The mental and physical health benefits of laughter are well documented. In a public health study conducted by a Dr Lee Berk in California, one hour of naturally induced laughter was demonstrated to boost your immune system by significantly lowering levels of the stress hormones, cortisol and epinephrine, and by increasing the production of T-cells, whose function is to defend you against infection.

Laughter, apart from making you and your date feel good, is excellent for promoting your wellbeing – studies have shown that after a good bout of laughter, your muscles loosen up and your heart rate and blood pressure are lowered, leaving you feeling more relaxed, calm and cheerful. Develop a keen eye for the absurd. If you look, you'll find that there are amusing absurdities a-plenty in life. Instead of letting a minor irritation or a petty upset annoy you, look for the funny side of life, and whenever you encounter it, laugh!

As you sit across the table looking into the eyes of your companion, remember these words from *Vanity Fair* by William Thackeray (1811–63):

> *'The world is a looking-glass, and gives back to every man the reflection of his own face. Frown at it, and it will in turn look sourly upon you; laugh at it and with it, and it is a jolly, kind companion.'*

If you and your companion succeed in getting a good laugh at some stage in your first date, you are off to a flying start! A shared sense of humour is an important element in any relationship.

Drink

Don't drink too much or too quickly. Control the temptation to knock back a few quickies in order to loosen up. It's always a good idea to have a bottle of water on the table, as well as the bottle of wine, to slow your alcohol intake. Countless promising romances end with the first date because one of the participants had too much to drink.

Paying

Going Dutch? Okay, but don't make a fuss if your date, either male or female, goes ahead and settles the bill. Now it is perfectly acceptable either way, but don't forget, chaps, most women like to be treated, just as they appreciate fresh and beautiful flowers and car doors being opened and closed for them.

Departure

Always understay your welcome on a first date unless you are very sure of what you are doing. Even if the date has gone exceedingly well and you are both up for more, it's far safer and more sensible to arrange to meet another time or to exchange telephone numbers, than risk a late nighter/all-nighter at this delicate stage, no matter how fabulous the prospect! Be the one to say 'Goodnight!' You'll be respected for that and if you both want to meet again, the chances are you will.

If things don't work out the way you'd hoped and there is to be no second date, although you might have wanted one, be graceful in the face of this disappointment. Dating is like that. In the early stages, you have good dates and disappointing ones. Very few people get it right first time. But you will succeed if you persevere; and you will persevere, because your goal is too magnificent to give up on.

Follow these basic but effective guidelines and there will be no stopping you. You will go from strength to strength (with perhaps, the occasional little hiccup along the way) until you find *the one*.

The Bottom Line

Relax, enjoy your dating experiences for this is your life and you shouldn't be afraid of it.

Compatibility

Experience shows us that love is not looking into one another's eyes but looking together in the same direction.

Antoine de Saint-Exupery 1900–44

Hopefully, you've had a few delicious dates. You've found someone special and you believe this one could be *the one*. Now, are you, or do you think you could be, compatible? Satisfy yourself that you both have a lot in common on a number of different levels. If not, each of you could find yourselves in different parts of the jungle, lobbing insults back and forth from either side of the living room!

Oh, but opposites attract! Yes, they do, but both parties to a relationship of opposites still need a lot in common, a number of shared interests, values, goals and ambitions that they can aspire to, embrace and celebrate together. Otherwise, they're not going to make it to magnificent twosomeness. In essence, being compatible means that you naturally tend to get on with each other. Although you may be very different, you both have similar or interrelated aims in life.

No matter how good the chemistry is between you, you'll find soon enough if you're hopelessly incompatible. If you cannot agree where to go, how to get there and what's going down when you arrive, it's clear you won't be together after a brief period of infatuation. Most couples discover within a few months if they are reasonably compatible, but without The Matchmaking Equation, it can take years, even decades, to discover if you're compatible enough to build a permanent future together.

Be careful here, though. On the one hand, we need to establish quickly and efficiently whether or not your new partner will shape up. On the other, we need to proceed carefully, so as not to appear obvious, pushy, or agenda-orientated. As the British novelist Thomas Hardy said, *'A lover without discretion is no lover at all.'* The last thing you want to do is to drive your new partner away through over-enthusiasm. It is extremely important to exercise restraint when sharing your hopes and dreams of a future together with the one you want. After all, people have a natural inclination to maintain their freedom and remain emotionally uncommitted until they themselves decide otherwise.

All relationships, during the delicate early stages – typically three weeks to six months – when they possess the potential to become permanent, or to expire at a moment's notice, require you to walk an exacting tightrope. You can't afford to allow yourself to be side-tracked down an emotional cul-de-sac by proceeding too cautiously, but you don't want your lover to do a runner because he or she feels pressurised and overwhelmed by you.

Make a note of the fact that no one runs from true love. They run from the fear of being cornered into something that they are not yet sure they want. Unless you allow sufficient time for your partner's feelings for you to nurture and grow, any premature threat to their freedom is likely produce psychological barriers of the 'Don't call me, I'll call you' variety. You must use delicacy and timing to probe and find out whether or not you and your new partner will be compatible in the long-term and you will need to establish this fact discreetly beyond all reasonable doubt within a period of three to nine months.

Most of us have cultural beliefs and values, even if we aren't necessarily conscious of them. We tend to feel comfortable with people whose views correspond very much with our own. Compatibility is firmly connected with past experiences and future expectations (and, sometimes, as a direct result of the limitations of these, with a desire to get away from the past and enliven the future).

It is the positive identification with someone who makes us feel relaxed to be with that sets the scene for compatibility. Usually, this is because there is ample capacity for sharing the common ground. That said, two people could still be compatible although their origins and life experiences would appear to set them apart.

The perceived wisdom of a thousand relationship books (I do not exaggerate) would seem to suggest there are certain key elements related to people's backgrounds that presuppose they are more likely to be compatible with some people rather than others. For instance, if you are courting someone of approximately the same age from a similar social, ethnic, religious and educational background, you are more likely to have the appropriate mix of characteristics that could combine to build long-term durability into a relationship.

But these characteristics are by no means the only indicators of probable compatibility. Other factors that can greatly influence the overall balance of harmony in a relationship include variable determinants like personal development and the study of how meaningful relationships work, along with the degree of conviction each partner holds that this relationship should be made to flourish and prosper.

Without doubt, the least visible and most critical aspects of compatibility to pinpoint and assess are the private dreams and expectations of each partner, because these are often held close to the heart. Some couples whose marriages collapse or whose relationships fall apart have been together for ages, without ever coming clean and discussing with each other their private dreams and expectations of life together. This will be by far the trickiest and most delicate area of compatibility to be teased out when the time comes to do the Matchmaking Equation in preparation for the Countdown at the end of the book.

Classic compatibility problems that crop up repeatedly in relationship counselling include significant age differences between partners, long-distance romances and widely differing social, ethnic, religious or educational backgrounds between the parties. I do not intend to warn you off such relationships because Tatiana and I share, or have encountered, all of the above differences in our relationship, which is thriving, like no other I have had before.

Instead of cautioning you, I propose to encourage you to concentrate on your strengths – those aspects of compatibility that excite you and unite you.

But first, you must be certain that you are not kidding yourself about what you do and do not have in common with your new partner. In order to find out how much real compatibility you enjoy in the relationship already, I want you to consider the list that follows, ticking the appropriate boxes to indicate either a 'Yes' answer or a known area of compatibility that exists between you.

I realise that you may have been dating for only a short period and some of the questions will strike you as premature at this early stage in the relationship. Simply skip those questions. Different relationships gain momentum at different paces. You can always return to this page in three to six months to complete the remaining blanks.

Compatibiliy confirmations

- Same social/ethnic background?

- Same religious background?

- Same educational background?

- Less than five years age differential?
- Do you live less than three hours' travelling time (door-to-door) apart?
- Do you enjoy each other's choice of restaurants, music, entertainment, etc?
- Do you share similar dreams, goals and ambitions?
- Can you make each other laugh?
- Are you at the same stage in your lives in terms of wanting to settle down?
- Do you appreciate each other's attitude to life in general?
- Can you handle each other's moods?
- Do you naturally gel together (most of the time)?
- Are you happy with the way you split routine chores?
- Do you agree about having/not having children in the future?
- Are you naturally supportive of each other?
- Do you have a basis for believing that you might have a future together?
- Do you tell each other the truth (excluding innocent little white lies)?
- Do you enjoy a good level of communication with each other most of the time?
- Do you have a workable mechanism for solving problems and resolving arguments?
- Do you both feel the need to put things right fast after an almighty ding-dong?

- Is each of you happy with the way the other handles their financial affairs?

- Do you have, or do you believe you will have, a satisfying sex life?

- Can you confirm that you are not hiding something important from your partner?

- Do you both feel able to discuss your innermost thoughts, desires and ambitions?

- Are you affectionate towards each other?

- Do you enjoy lengthy, lazy, talkative meals at home with each other?

- Do you indulge your partner with impromptu treats or surprises?

- Are you both sure that each of you wants a meaningful, long-term relationship?

- Do you agree, or, if it is premature to ask, are you are likely to agree on family matters, etc?

- Do you have any special hobbies or pastimes you enjoy participating in together?

- Are you each comfortable with the way the other looks, dresses, talks and touches you?

- Do you both put time and effort into keeping the relationship fresh and exciting?

- Do you get on well with each other's relatives, friends and children (if applicable)?

- Do you feel that there is a healthy, reasonably equal balance of power in the relationship?

Now, before reading on, I want you to list, in order of importance to you personally, the six most significant things you have in common with your new partner.

Did you find it easy to write down six? Could you readily have included more? Good! Things are going in the right direction. Or did you find it difficult? If you had to struggle to find six, I think you'll know that it's not good news. Perhaps it's time for a rethink.

But, you say, the sex is great! I want to stay with... *Be warned.* That's lust and infatuation. Great while it lasts. But it's not going to last. Enjoy what you're getting if that's what you want but don't fool yourself into thinking you're having a relationship in the proper sense of the word. Keep your brain clear.

I am not saying it's easy to back off. You may feel that this person has enough to offer to justify you taking a risk and that if you give him/her up there may be no one else. Should you decide to go ahead against the signals, I genuinely wish you luck and happiness, but be aware that the chances are you'll break up in due course and someone's heart will be broken. It could be yours.

 ## *The Bottom Line*

The more you have in common with your partner, the more potential the relationship has.

169

Emotional availability

The mind is its own place,
And in itself can make A heaven of Hell, a hell of Heaven.

Paradise Lost, John Milton 1608–74

Wow! You've been dating steadily for a while now. You've established that you have much in common and you're convinced that you are, or could be, compatible. The chemistry is there and the two of you spark! It all seems so right and you seriously believe that this one really could be the one.

This person whom you are on the verge of falling in love with, is he or she emotionally available for you? If not, no matter how strongly you feel, you're wasting your time, you won't get the emotional support you deserve when you need it the most. Over time, when the relationship is under strain, you'll become aware of an emotional time warp: the pair of you will be in two different emotional time zones! The right partner at the wrong time is the wrong partner for you right now.

The right partner at the right time is the only partner for you because the emotional availability of both parties to a relationship is a prerequisite for a happy and lasting relationship. You cannot make it to magnificent twosomeness if your partner is perfect in every way, except that he or she is emotionally unavailable for you.

I have been emotionally unavailable to every woman, pre-Tatiana, who ever entered my life, including two wonderful ex-wives. Nobody could ever change that because emotional non-availability is something that only the individual concerned can deal with. I sorted myself out before Tatiana came into my life full time. When I told you, in Part 1 that writing a mission statement can have an empowering effect, I wasn't kidding!

So many promising relationships are stillborn because one partner is simply not emotionally available for any meaningful relationship. They can't help it, they don't necessarily realise that they have a problem. This has nothing to do with commitment; it has everything to do with emotional blockages leading right back to childhood, or some other deeply rooted emotional trauma.

The important point to note here is that emotional damage is frequently beyond the scope of any partner, no matter how loving. The person who is emotionally blocked must be avoided at all costs by anyone wanting a permanent relationship. It's up to the emotionally damaged individual to seek the appropriate professional help and diagnosis and to undergo an effective course of therapy, before he or she will ever be fit to embrace a loving relationship that lasts.

Is your new partner emotionally available to you most of the time or is he or she emotionally shut down? Warning signs to look for include:

Your partner:

- Has difficulty showing emotion
- Has difficulty talking about his or her feelings
- Will not be completely open with you
- Cannot trust you

- Harbours anger and resentment towards one or both of their parents or an ex

- Is addicted to alcohol, illegal drugs, or substances

- Has fits of rage and sometimes behaves in an irrational or violent manner.

Incidentally, if you always seem to attract the type of person who is emotionally unavailable, you might want to question why! Could it be that a part of you feels at home in this environment? Are you simply unlucky, or could you be a prime candidate for therapy yourself?

Don't panic!
It's quite possible you have identified warning signs in your new partner – and possibly in yourself. This is not necessarily the end. Depending on how you see the overall position, it could be a new starting point. Talk to your partner, acknowledge the problem and discuss possible solutions. If you need specialist hands-on professional help, work it out together at a relationship workshop. This process will increase your understanding and respect for each other. If this is not the case, if you can't handle it, there is doubt about your immaturity as a pair and maybe the way ahead is closing.

There is another – less serious but still potentially terminal – form of emotional non-availability and this is predominantly to do with timing. For example, if any of the following situations sound uncomfortably close to home in your new relationship, alarm bells should be ringing.

Your partner:

- Has reached a critical stage in his or her career

- Has only recently come out of another serious, long-term relationship

- Has unfinished business with an ex

- Is married/divorcing/contemplating a divorce
- Simply isn't ready for a serious relationship yet.

Still don't panic!

Work through. Don't necessarily assume – even if your partner appears to be more mature than you are – that he or she knows how to proceed progressively to a deeper and more meaningful relationship with you.

There are few things more frustrating in life than thinking you have found *the one* only to find that he or she could indeed be your ideal partner *if only* the timing was different. We've already dealt with the *if only* scenario earlier in the book so you know exactly what you have to do if you don't see things working out to your mutual satisfaction sooner rather than later.

Timing is not all bad news. It's just that now is the time to be aware if your partner is unlikely to go the distance due to emotional non-availability or bad timing – before you get in too deep! The majority of couples who get together do so because the timing is right.

The timing was certainly right for David Bowie, the iconic rock star from Brixton, and Iman, the Muslim Somali supermodel, when they were set up on a blind date organised by the Los Angeles hairdresser Teddy Antolin.

'*It was so lucky that we were to meet at that time in our lives, when we were both yearning for each other,*' says Bowie. They met in 1990 when they were both at an emotional low and ever since Mr and Mrs Bowie have been regarded as one of the most loving of showbiz couples.

 The Bottom Line

> The timing must be right for romance and you must be emotionally available for each other.

The one for you

*Women don't look for handsome men; they look
for men with beautiful women.*

Milan Kundera

The one for you means exactly what it says – *the one for you*. Not the one everybody else ogles over, or the one that your mum, your dad, your best friend or the editor of *Cosmopolitan* or *Playboy* magazine believes to be right for you.

We are talking here about the person who is going to take you as near to heaven as you can get to on this earth. Never commit yourself to a relationship with someone else's fantasy. Most of these were manufactured in some Hollywood or Bollywood studio, TV soap, fashion house PR department, or at the whim of some power-hungry media mogul who wouldn't recognise true love if it presented itself on the front page – not unless it was celebrity-related or advertising-sponsored.

The need for approval of your partner in somebody else's eyes must play no part in your decision of who is right for you.

Find someone who will fulfil your needs, someone who genuinely wants to make you happy. There can be no denying that tangible things like money, fame, good looks and material prospects play their part in almost everybody's choice of the perfect partner, but lasting satisfaction involves more than this.

Don't confuse this critical appraisal of consumer interests and the validity of other people's input with the Asian culture and the Orthodox Jewish tradition of arranged marriages. These – as opposed to forced marriages – are unions based on the mutual interests of both parties and take into account religious beliefs, personal aspirations and levels of education, rather than relying on physical attraction to bring the couple together in the first place.

This system, when properly applied, is not as draconian as some might imagine. Arranged marriages are simply introductions: the element of choice remains. True, initial meetings between would-be brides and grooms take place in front of their families, but subsequent dates are usually unchaperoned. Typically, no decisions are expected until at least the sixth meeting, and by then most people can form an opinion as to whether or not they have enough in common to make a success of marriage, perhaps leading on to magnificent twosomeness.

If you are dating someone who makes your eyes lock, your heart pound and your knees tremble and cave in beneath you just by thinking about them, you know you have been struck by the thunderbolt of lust, and passion isn't an issue for you.

But not everyone is struck that way when they first realise that they are falling for someone. In any event, whether love hits you between the eyes and knocks you senseless, or creeps up on you gradually and takes you by stealth almost against your will, the time has come to ask yourself the key question: is this the one? Mr or Ms Absolutely Right in the flesh?

The only way to find out is to consider coolly and dispassionately here and now how you feel when you're with this person. Do you feel relaxed, comfortable, excited, turned on, happy and enthusiastic about your future? Can you be open and totally frank with each other?

Is it fun, uplifting and easy to be together? Do you share, or, if not, are you tolerant towards each other's views and values – emotionally, physically, economically and spiritually? Do you respect each other? When you quarrel, as you will, do you feel the need to make up, because you can't stand the pain of seeing your partner, and yourself, hurt? Are you both naturally moving in the same direction in life? Are there lots of different things you enjoy discussing and doing together? Do you share the same aspirations?

If you're answering 'Yes' to a lot of questions, things are beginning to look good, very good, but with the Countdown method, we leave nothing to chance. Let's do something lovers and potential lovers seldom do: let's get technical! Put aside for now the feelings of our heart and examine seven crucial qualities, all of which your partner will need to possess or develop to ensure long-term potential for a permanent and rewarding relationship with you.

Passion: The laws of attraction dictate that your partner must do it for you! This doesn't mean to say that you have to break out in red-hot flushes at the mere mention of their name. It does mean that you cannot fake it, deny your true feelings or kid yourself. You have to believe that this person will love you like no other, in the way that you want to be loved, and you have to know that you want to love this person, with overwhelming passion, no holding back and with no strings attached!

A mistake many of us make when looking for the ideal partner is to assume that there must be instant attraction, rather than a gradual one. If you meet someone eligible but you are not necessarily attracted to him or her straightaway, it doesn't mean that you won't become attracted to this person as you get to know them better.

Sharing your thoughts, feelings and experiences with one another often results in strong mental and emotional resonance that can spark physical attraction and sexual resonance. This is the basis upon which professionally arranged marriages are put together. Generally, they work because attraction is based upon how you feel about yourself when the two of you are together, taking into account your respective backgrounds and future expectations, not simply physical attraction in the first instance.

Positive attitude: Is the glass half-full or half-empty? And, does it make the slightest bit of difference? Well, yes, rather a lot, actually. Admittedly, this is not the sort of question one ponders in the early stages of a relationship, but whether your partner has an essentially positive view of the world, rather than a negative one, will make a big difference to your quality of life.

High self-esteem: This is conducive to a healthy, loving relationship because realistically, if your partner knows how to treat himself or herself well, there is a firm basis for believing that he or she will know how to treat you well too. People with low self-esteem often need someone to love to be able to feel good about themselves, whereas people with high self-esteem are secure within themselves and when they give their love, it's because they really want to.

Personal integrity: This is paramount to the long-term success of a relationship in this dangerous, tricky, over-hyped and increasingly crass environment in which we live. Do you really want to spend the rest of your life with someone who doesn't have the courage of his or her own convictions? Most of us perpetrate the occasional borderline naughty, but can you really admire someone who is as straightforward as a spin-doctor? Remember – there are people out there who would not think twice about taking advantage of you when the opportunity presents itself.

Emotional maturity: This quality is conducive to a relaxed and open relationship where feelings can be expressed and shared, and problems – even matters of an intimate nature – can be tackled together in a positive and supportive environment. Successful intimate relationships are not based on sharing bricks-and-mortar, a king-size bed and a luxury bathroom. They are based on shared emotions.

Relationship-orientated partners: Naturally 'we' people, rather than 'I' individuals tend to be adaptive and forward looking, responding easily to changes as the relationship grows and matures, seeking knowledge and enlightenment to steer both parties on to a greater a more fulfilling lifetime of shared experiences. These are the people who understand the value of personal and partnership growth. To make it to magnificent twosomeness, it's helpful to be the partner, or to have a partner, with commitment to mutual growth.

A kind and responsive nature: This is not necessarily fashionable or very available in this age of advantage-taking and humiliation of all things gentle. But, when it comes to settling down and cuddling up close – through the good times as well as the real downers – you'll appreciate this very special quality.

In conclusion, it's worth noting that all of the above seven qualities – *yes, all of them* – can be cultivated. Go ahead and choose the partner for you with the full confidence and courage of your convictions. Use your head, your heart and your gut instinct to guide you to Mr or Ms Absolutely Right. It's your call!

 The Bottom Line

> The one for you is the person you choose of your own free will.

CHAPTER 7

PART
4

The moment – don't let it escape

Take time to deliberate, but when the time for action has arrived, stop thinking and jump in.

Napoleon Bonaparte 1769–1821

This chapter is short because I have only one message to give you and I can deliver it here and now to maximum effect on an otherwise blank page. When the time comes, and it will, you will know the moment I am referring to: that magical, defining moment when you have both the opportunity and the desire to do something or say something that seems so right. This moment defines your character and opens a whole new world for two. Don't let it escape because this moment will never be that perfect again.

 ## The Bottom Line

Cupid helps those who help themselves.
Remember that when your magic moment comes.

PART 5

Romance

Yes, it will be bliss
To go with you by train to Diss,
Your walking shoes upon your feet;
We'll meet, my sweet,
at Liverpool Street

Sir John Betjeman
1906–84

CHAPTER 1

PART
5

That loving feeling

*In the final analysis of our lives – when the to-do lists are no
more and the frenzy is over – the only thing that'll have value is
whether we've loved others, and whether they've loved us.*

Oprah Winfrey

The essence of that loving feeling is closeness. Intimate, satisfying
closeness that can only be achieved over time, through shared
experience and an ever-increasing coming together of two loving
people.

So many immortal words – in music, theatre, books, poems and
drama – have been written on love and love-related themes that I
see no value in adding to them. Instead, I will attempt to break
down the mystery of that loving feeling, bearing in mind we are
dealing with a topic that baffles much of the world's population
most of the time.

That loving feeling comes into being when you are captivated
by someone, when you lose yourself in the moment, letting go of
your inhibitions, your doubts and any lingering feelings of anxiety
long enough to allow your senses to come alive and vividly express
themselves. Whenever the mind focuses on something wonderful,
it relaxes, and when the mind relaxes, all the little paranoid

thoughts that we are prone to – *Do you really like me? Am I intelligent or beautiful enough? What does the future hold?* – vanish from the surface and you feel great.

That loving feeling re-establishes your sense of worth and your zest for life and goes from strength to strength when you stop thinking in terms of you and him, or me and her, and start interacting as we.

Have you noticed how some couples are much more of a couple than others? The expressions *'They're so close'*, *'they're an item'*, *'they're so much in love'* point to a special quality that is more than the sum of the two individuals taken together. Some definite process – that loving feeling – has taken hold of them and brought about a transformation. There is a distinct sense of we about them, a close bond and a perception that they have something most of us don't and this presence makes itself known wherever they are. How did they achieve that? In this part of the book, we shall find out.

The Bottom Line

The essence of that loving feeling is closeness, no matter where in the world you are.

CHAPTER 2

PART
5

Sex – lighting an inextinguishable fire

Is that a pistol in your pocket, or are you just glad to see me?

Mae West 1892–1980

I'm a great believer in the notion that if you are going to do something, do it with style! Do it with an almighty bang no matter how much extra effort this takes to accomplish. Making love to your partner – which I shall refer to as sex – is a wonderful landscape on which to colour this theme because if you're good together in bed, you will be receptive to getting even better. If you don't rate yourself very highly, you'll be relieved to learn that with a little bit of theatre, the element of surprise and some guidance and understanding, you can quickly improve your performance and enjoyment of sex.

Desire is the most delicate ingredient in sex. Part of it is chemistry; a complex cocktail of developmental and hormonal factors that makes you fancy one person and not another, and regulates when you want to have sex with that person and when you do not. This chemistry, most of the time, is automatic and it is either there from the start of a relationship or not. But there are exceptions: people have been known to fancy a friend (of either sex) or someone who they previously never saw as a potential sexual partner, months, or even years, after they first met them.

The right chemistry gives a powerful kick-start to any sexual relationship, but it is by far the most fragile element. Sex does not start downstairs but upstairs in the brain. This means that images and fantasies can also stir desire, regardless of whether or not you happen to be with your partner at the time.

There is an element of fantasy in any new relationship that makes for a high level of desire at the beginning. This invariably peaks and settles at a more sustainable level in relationships that build the momentum and durability to last a lifetime. But there are other chemical triggers like love itself, admiration, pleasure in each other's company, comfort, trust, respect, intellectual rapport, courtesy and compromise and other positive links that feed desire.

In contrast, anger, disappointment, misery, insecurity, mistrust, lack of communication and other relationship problems usually have the effect of reducing desire for sex in women, but not necessarily in men. Even difficulties not directly related with the relationship, like exhaustion from excessive work, stress-related travel difficulties, including, perhaps, the fact that she reversed the car into a tree, can have the effect of putting the brakes on a woman's sex drive. Whereas a man, in similar circumstances, is more likely to see the opportunity for sex as welcome and the aftermath of sex as a sleeping pill – an effective way of releasing the accumulated aggravation and tensions of the day.

The final factor in maintaining high levels of desire is the quality of sex itself. Knowing how, when best and where in particular to arouse each other sexually to give maximum satisfaction is a major ingredient in arousing desire. Master that and you will light an inextinguishable fire in the brain of your partner.

Satisfying both yourself and your partner isn't a luxury, it's almost essential for the long-term and healthy survival of your relationship. Sex is good for us, both physically and mentally. It lowers stress levels, increases the amount of quality sleep, boosts the immune system, generates a tremendous sense of affinity with your partner through intimacy, and, done properly, is enjoyable in the extreme.

But how do we do it right on a regular basis when men's and women's sexual needs and desires can be so different – changeable through different cycles of the relationship – and affected by extraordinary factors like babies, prescription drugs, growing older and the menopause?

The place to start is to understand the differences between men and women when it comes to sex. From that point, we can learn by experimentation how to please our partner right from the outset. We need to because how a man feels during the act of making love to a new partner is of prime importance to him, but how a woman feels the morning after making love to her new partner can be especially poignant to her. In finding out how to please, we will probably discover that we are willingly given much more of what we want in return – in the way that we like it – and that the occasional hiccup in performance (which we all suffer) is more easily forgotten.

A major characteristic of couples who are happy and contented in love is that they view sex as an expression of intimacy and they don't take exception to any differences in their needs or desires. Let's take a closer look at these different needs and desires so that we can figure out how to satisfy them.

When you get right down to it, the most striking distinction between the sexes is that women need a lot of preparation, pampering and gentle foreplay before they're ready for sex whereas men, when erect, like to get stuck in without delay.

Guys, you know perfectly well that a diesel engine won't perform brilliantly from cold. Well, in bed, she's the diesel (complete with the noise, hopefully) and you're the petrol variant. Ladies, I know that you always heat the oven before preparing a magnificent dish, whereas you can shove a hot dog in the microwave and expect some immediate action. In sexual warm-up terms, you're the magnificent dish and he's the dog.

From a cold start to orgasm, a healthy man can come in approximately the time it takes to boil an egg. For a healthy woman, she would ideally prefer five or six times that – about the time it takes to prepare all the fresh ingredients, complete with a delicious side salad and home-made dressing, and cook an omelette to perfection. It will not have escaped your notice that more of the time for this particular culinary delight is consumed in preparation of the dish than in the heat of the pan!

No other area of a couple's life offers more potential for embarrassment, hurt and rejection than sex. No wonder couples find it challenging to discuss the subject at all, let alone objectively! Men are stimulated through their eyes, women through their ears. Men's brains are wired to look at the contours of a woman's body, and this is why erotic images have so much impact on them. Women, with their greater range of sensory information receptors, want to hear sweet words. So great is a woman's need to hear comforting words, reassuring compliments and sweet nothings from her man that she may even close her eyes to intensify and more deeply experience this element of this pre-sex eroticism. By contrast, what men want from sex is simple: the release of pent-up tension by climaxing and releasing their sperm.

A woman has different priorities: she needs to experience the steady build-up of pleasure over a significantly longer period. He wants to empty – she wants to be filled. Understanding the different priorities of the sexes is the single most important facilitator in becoming a caring lover. Most women need at least

30 minutes of foreplay before they are ready for sex. Men, 30 seconds will suffice.

As a man it's extremely likely that you can experience sexual arousal and climax with consummate ease. This is not always the case with women, because before their emotional needs are met they can't willingly respond physically. Men, understandably, find it hard to respond emotionally when their physical needs have yet to be met, but it's very much in their interest to learn to understand and satisfy their partner's emotional needs. When they do, the woman in their life is likely to respond in a way that they never dreamed possible.

The most powerful single piece of knowledge that a man can possess about how to turn a woman on is to know that a woman is receptive to making love only when her emotional needs have been met.

A woman becomes marvellous in bed when you let her know that she's special, very much appreciated and loved with an intensity that no other man could manage. In the run-up to making love you must give her your undivided attention, demonstrating that you care by showing her lots of little kindnesses in words and gentle caresses.

The moment she removes (or you remove) her bra and pants is worthy of comment – and a flattering one at that! After all, she may well have put them on especially for you. How is she expected to feel if you didn't even notice what she was wearing before she stripped naked, let alone the colour, the texture, the style, the shape and the feel of the lingerie that is no more? Remember, a woman will not necessarily be in the mood to make love just because you are up for it and strategically in position. She'll be in the mood because you are nice to her.

So many people feel vulnerable about whether or not they appear attractive, sexy and a good lover in the eyes of their partner that it is a good idea to be gentle and constructive when talking about sex. A lovemaking session that starts with one party criticising the other is going to end faster than the quickest of quickies.

Nothing is guaranteed to make your partner embrace you less than if you say, 'You never hold me tenderly!' It is better to say, 'I loved it when we made love in the leather armchair the night before and you ran your fingers through my hair before putting your arms around me. I'd love more of that. It makes me feel so good.' Likewise, instead of saying 'Don't touch me there!' you'll get a better response if you say something like, 'It feels so sensuous when you touch me here,' guiding their hand to the spot that does it for you. When you talk to your partner about sex, your approach should always be one of wishing to make a good thing better. Even if your sex life is disappointing, you need to accentuate the positive in order to work towards a more satisfying outcome. That means learning the right way to ask for what you want and the appropriate way to react to your partner's requests.

If you are on the receiving end of your partner's request, try very hard to avoid seeing it as an implied criticism of yourself, your actions or any lack of action. Make a point of adopting a positive attitude towards what is being suggested. After all, you both want a great sex life and this involves not only experimentation, but also a little give and take from each other. Should your partner ask if you would like to freshen up, clean your teeth and give your mouth a rinse, this is not the type of request you consider. You just do it! Some people feel uncomfortable talking about sex in the run-up to making love. If this sounds like you, try discussing any aspects of lovemaking that are important to you before you get undressed. Talking about sex can often make for some interesting foreplay.

Most men are reluctant to admit that there might be something they should know about a woman's body that they don't know, but if you want to be able to truly please a woman in bed, you have got to know the functions of the parts you're dealing with.

The G-spot is a well-known point of confusion for men. It's not a buried treasure somewhere deep in the nooks and crannies of the vagina, it is located on the front wall of the vagina, an inch or two inside. If you put your index finger just inside the vagina and gently pull towards you with a 'follow me' motion, you should be able to pinpoint her G-spot. It feels different from the rest of the vaginal wall, very slightly elevated and softer to the touch.

Few men use their fingers to lovingly explore their partners' bodies. Many kiss and go straight for her knickers, taking a short detour over her breasts if they are that way inclined. If you spend time touching her, stroking her, massaging her, loving her entire body, the overall sensation of sex that you both experience will be elevated to a higher level of pleasure as you perfect the art of foreplay.

Most men are good with their hands when it comes to practical matters, but a man with an accomplished pair of hands in the bedroom is a potential champion to be groomed for stardom. Although this is not the classic film or TV image, most women prefer graduated petting – from light to heavy – before being penetrated, rather than a quick thrust!

Every woman is different. Some like it when their breasts are touched lightly; others cringe when they are squeezed. Many women like having their breasts kneaded and firmly squeezed, but heaven help the man that squeezes too hard. A squeal is hard to interpret. Is it pleasure or is it painful? Does she like pleasure and nothing more, or does she prefer her pleasure laced with pain? If you are not sure, ask.

Until you find out what drives her completely out of her mind, proceed slowly, don't take risks and err on the side of tenderness. Listen to the subtle hints she gives you, read her body language, follow the clues and you will be heading for a sex life greater and more fulfilling than you ever dreamed in your wildest dreams. Some men assume – sometimes correctly, sometimes not – that deliciously hard and erect nipples mean she's warming to what is coming, but she might be simply nervous or cold. It's also important to understand that nipples and breasts enlarge in the days before a woman's period. Your partner's breasts will desire different types of titillation at different times of her monthly cycle. The man who understands this and responds accordingly is the champion who walks off with all the accolades and is the male contingent of a magnificent twosome-to-be.

Just as men applaud a woman who enjoys sucking them senseless, women really appreciate a man who enjoys going down to lick and probe where it matters the most. When you go down on a woman, it's about a whole lot more than just an orgasm or three; it's about moving the ends of the Earth for which you are in pivotal control. If you start, you must give your woman the total satisfaction she needs to worship you to and beyond your dying day.

Since a woman's centre of pleasure is her clitoris, oral sex is a sure way for her to reach orgasm. Be prepared to go the distance and she'll explode in a mind-blowing climax!

Some people, men and women, simply don't derive pleasure from going down. That's okay, never feel obliged to do what you don't want to do, but remember – many of the great things in life are acquired tastes. Did you enjoy wine the very first time you tasted it?

Ladies, now that your man has learned to prepare you for the ultimate sexual experience, the time has come to despatch your man to heaven. You should use provocative and time-consuming-to-remove accessories to slow his need to penetrate you at the earliest opportunity. Stockings and suspenders slip tantalisingly to mind in the eyes of most men – particularly if they are red or black and glimpsed through a slit skirt so that the psychological and practical elements of conquest remain – no matter how familiar he is with you. Yes, I know that pink or cream is the preferred colour of many women, but unless you're seducing a lesbian lover, stick to the colours suggested!

It may be that this type of display would only make you shy and inhibited. That's okay. Forget it. The majority of men will delay taking you in 10 seconds flat if you massage their scalp in the manner of an authentic Indian head massage. Coincidentally, this is believed to have the added benefit of delaying premature baldness because it stimulates the flow of blood to the follicles of his hair, but this is probably not on your mind at the moment! If you have long nails, try gently scratching his scalp, then slowly working your way down the back of his scalp, his neck bone and the full length of his spine until you reach and probe the sensitive part of his ass with the slightest touch of your fingernails.

If you're thinking of giving your man a right royal taste of oral sex, start by sucking on his fingers to give him a hint of what might be coming his way. Don't forget to look him straight in the eyes as you drive him to distraction – you'll be demonstrating that you're a woman who clearly delights in giving as good as she gets when the mood takes you.

When you get down to the real thing, run your thumb over the most sensitive part of his penis – this is the tip where the parting lips can be persuaded to open out to greet you. Manually stimulate him before licking, running your tongue up and down the full length of his cock, which you will observe thickening, hardening and expanding before your very eyes. Pay particular attention to the corona – the ridge that runs all the way round the head of the penis (not on all men) because the majority of men find this reef particularly sensitive.

Stroking the shaft with a steady rhythm will usually do the trick of preparing him for what's to come, before putting his cock in your mouth, sucking and maybe swallowing everything your man has to offer. Or perhaps you have other ideas. Maybe you are merely preparing him for the main event and when you are ready you will open your legs and guide him to the perfect docking procedure. In the unlikely event that there is any reluctance to succumb to your will, tantalise the sack of his balls – called the scrotum – in the palm of one hand and delicately stroke this susceptible area with the upturned index finger of the other hand.

Occasionally, in my experience of stress management – even with the finest of bedfellows and the most loving of women – there are difficulties of a sexual nature that need attention. The biggest single leap forward to resolving any problem of sexual dysfunction is to admit that there is one and seek an immediate remedy.

Understandably, many people, particularly men, feel awkward and reluctant to talk about sexual problems and difficulties. Sometimes you can ignore them or simply forget about them, and they melt away of their own accord. If the problem persists, you need the help of the professionals, commencing with an on-the-ball diagnosis. If you have the support and the encouragement of your partner at this difficult time, it can mean so much. If you're not sure where to seek help, start with your medical practitioner. In the vast majority of cases, he or she will be able give you an accurate diagnosis within 10 minutes and prescribe, or suggest, a remedy. Alternatively, your doctor may refer you to a qualified sex therapist. The three most common libido killers – all of which can be resolved – are: depression, high blood pressure and stress.

Depression: While depression itself often causes loss of desire, it is ironic that low libido and impaired orgasm in both men and women are common side-effects of the increasingly popular anti-depressants known as selective serotonin reuptake inhibitors (SSRIs), known more commonly as Prozac or Seroxat.

Seven out of ten women are unable to reach orgasm on these drugs and almost half of all men and women report sexual dysfunction. Although these drugs serve a useful purpose, many people stay on them for far too long. The obvious solution, if your only existing problem is sex related, is to consult your doctor with a view to gradually reducing your dosage and weaning yourself off the drugs altogether. If you need practical guidance on how to cope with depression, read my book, *Beat Depression*, published by Hodder and Stoughton.

High blood pressure: Certain types of prescription drugs that lower your blood pressure, such as beta-blockers, are a common cause of impotency and sexual dysfunction because they relax the blood vessels that need to constrict during erection and arousal. Consult your doctor about a possible review/change in medication. Having experienced hypertension (very high blood pressure) on one side of my body and low blood pressure on the other – abnormal in the extreme – this is a problem I have encountered and long-since overcome. For practical guidance on high blood pressure, see my book, *After Stroke*, published by Thorsons.

Stress: Give yourselves a break away from the stresses and strains of modern-day living. Take an extended holiday or, if time is prohibitive, a weekend break. Before you set off, make a firm and binding commitment with your partner that neither of you will bring up or even mention your problems while you're chilling out.

Relax and enjoy quality time together, pampering yourselves in the luxury of a romantic hotel or, if you prefer, the peace and quiet of a holiday cottage or caravan in the middle of nowhere, on the coast or in some picture postcard location. When you truly relax, the chances are that the two of you will feel closer and more intimate and you will find yourselves making love so emotional and satisfying that you sleep deeper and sweeter than you did at home.

When you awake, you may discover that the problem you didn't bring with you has assumed a lower profile, resolved itself, or one of you has come up with the perfect solution. Am I being wildly optimistic? No, when you relax and chill out together, things usually come right in the end. That's the beauty of togetherness, so invest time and effort in lighting an inextinguishable sexual fire between you and feel the glowing heat of never-ending passion.

The Bottom Line

Sex: what is it for you – the be all and end all of the moment, or the expression of a loving partnership?

CHAPTER 3

PART
5

Power shift – dancing on the escalator

Instead of seeing the rug being pulled from under us,
we can learn to dance on the shifting carpet.

Thomas F Crumb

Imagine this scene. You and your beloved are in a busy underground station at the height of the morning rush hour. You've been parted in the crush between the platform and the exit that is accessed by a parallel pair of up-escalators.

You find yourself on one and your partner – no more than two arm-lengths away – is on the other, directly opposite and moving in the same direction as you are at the same speed. You smile at each other, then strangely, your escalator experiences a power shift, speeding up and leaving your partner behind, before stopping altogether so that once again your partner is level with you, and then progressing ahead, leaving you behind.

Life is a bit like that. If your relationship is to make it to a higher level in the long term, you'll need to be able to negotiate power shifts and to dance on the moving escalator of life. This chapter alerts you to some likely hazards, just as a red light signals danger ahead.

Relationship danger spots that we are going to immunise ourselves against with a quick short jab of reality include:

1 Power struggle

2 Power shift

3 Post-commitment

4 Baby

5 Grief

6 Work-related stress.

Power struggle
Power struggles can be a major stumbling block in relationships that have made it to the commitment stage, or ones that are moving in that direction. When couples do not know how to resolve their power struggles, they end up quarrelling and using all sorts of means – both above-board and devious – to impose their will and get their way. In effect, they are competing with their own partner for power and influence within the relationship.

When both partners understand the dynamics of power struggles, it is much easier to reach an accommodation that will recognise and satisfy the legitimate needs of each. Left to go on unchecked, power struggles, after causing a lot of argument and distress between the partners who each have their own priorities and want to do things their way, will result in a winner/loser situation and the relationship itself is ultimately lost.

The only way to excel and move towards magnificent twosomeness in any relationship is to accept that power struggles happen, they're healthy and natural; but a win-win situation must be created or both parties lose. This is achieved through the realisation that both parties are equal and the proper recognition of their interests is essential to the long-term success of any loving relationship.

Of course, there are bound to be elements of unevenness in any relationship, but these should be balanced and accepted by both parties as fair and reasonable. Abiding friendship, trust, tolerance, understanding and respect for each other needs to be established before a healthy win-win state of equilibrium can result and the all-embracing elasticity of a lasting relationship achieved.

Power shift

The most common type of power shift is when one partner is promoted at work, or lands a new job with a huge increase in salary. At first, both partners are overjoyed and celebrate. Later, tension can start to creep in. The partner that hasn't had the increase or the promotion may begin to feel (or be made to feel) inferior, the one who has, superior. There may be a shift in expectations.

At times like this, it's important to recognise that you each bring different but equally valuable qualities to the relationship. Money-wise, renegotiate the financial arrangements between you to avoid resentment but don't be tempted to use financial power to control the relationship. The key factor here for the health of the relationship is flexibility. Remember, neither money nor status can guarantee success or happiness in love. If they could, all millionaires would be happy, and lords and ladies of the realm and the stars of TV and film would live happily ever after.

Post-commitment

As with many of the major lifestyle decisions in life, there comes a time for many people when they have second thoughts, a few months or years down the line, about whether they have done the right thing. It's a natural phenomenon partly connected with the power struggle when you realise that you have surrendered some of the pleasing aspects of being single in deference to your partner: territorial, domestic and independence issues, like doing what you want, when you want, where you want and how you want to, without the need to consider anybody else spring to mind.

At times like this, the benefits of a committed partnership are not at the forefront of your mind and you tend to dwell on what you've lost, not the tremendous benefits of what you have gained. In a healthy relationship, this is merely a passing phase and is helped by making time to see friends and colleagues and pursuing interests and hobbies of your own. Living together doesn't necessarily mean doing absolutely everything together. Make sure you each have your own personal space at home where you can relax with your private thoughts within the security of a loving relationship.

Take the heat out of the kitchen and the housework by sharing the burden. Have clear areas or days of responsibility, or do things together while you chat and have fun. Make cooking an enjoyable part of your evening together. Couples who take the trouble to talk to each other over a leisurely meal, perhaps with a glass of wine or something else to prolong the pleasure, resolve issues more easily and derive more enjoyment from their meals at home.

Baby

Despite the undoubted joys of parenthood, this is a particularly demanding time for new parents and they need high levels of support and co-operation from each other. The happiness factor of an otherwise good relationship can implode because of reduced sleep, lack of sex and the fact that the man of the house is playing a secondary role to a baby.

It's crucial at this time that you have grown-up conversations about each other's concerns and don't simply talk about the baby. Kindness, understanding and patience will be at a premium now because, understandably, change is hard for you both. At least once a week arrange for the baby's grandparents to give you a break, get your friends to cover or arrange a baby-sitter for the evening. Never forget that the two of you are special; you're not just parents – you're a devoted couple and you need time to relax, time to go out together and have a good time, and time for uninterrupted sex!

Grief

When someone dear to you dies, you might expect grief to bring you and your partner closer together. Sometimes it does, but not always. It can have the effect of driving a wedge between you. For the bereaved person, the world can suddenly become a lonely, unfamiliar place. The experience can be shattering for the bereaved person's partner as well. They can feel excluded, left out from all the grief, their sympathy and willingness to comfort seemingly rejected.

It helps to understand that the bereaved person will need to be with family and friends at this difficult time. Their partner must be satisfied with a supporting role and should try not to feel shut out. Whether it's you or your partner who is bereaved, it's comforting to know that a strong relationship can be a reminder that life goes on.

Work-related stress

Make no mistake, in this modern world where computers are supposed to take the strain, if we are determined to succeed – in business, working for a branch of government, a charitable or commercial organisation, large or small – we have to work like never before or we are history. This is a recipe for stress, along with the hardship caused by involuntary unemployment, and the potential for upset where one partner is employed and the other is not.

The secret of success for determined magnificent twosomes-to-be is to make time for your partner, no matter how tired and exhausted you may be. Listen to their complaints, their protestations, their successes, even if you are so tired you fall asleep in the act. Demonstrate that you care and you will love and support them through thick and thin, although you might be treading water and struggling yourself. This is the stuff of great love affairs and you don't have to be magnificent to achieve it, you just have to be you.

The Bottom Line

In smoothing out the bumps caused by power shifts, make sure you don't become complacent.

Fighting and making up

If I were your wife, I would poison your coffee.

If I were your husband, I would drink it.

Nancy Astor 1879–1964, Winston Churchill 1874–1965

No one in his or her right mind wants to have a right ding-dong with their loved one, but providing the warring parties can bring themselves to make up promptly afterwards – before resentment sets in and festers – it is an effective way of clearing the air.

The word 'fight' means different things to different people depending on their age, sex and upbringing. The same word can mean different things at different times to the same person, depending on their mood and the amount of alcohol they have consumed. For the purpose of clarity, we will understand it to mean a domestic quarrel, a heated verbal argument and a right royal row without violence of any kind – although some couples, in the heat of the moment – get physical as well. Of course, it is preferable not to fight at all. Nevertheless, it is possible to have a wonderful relationship and fight with your lover from time to time. Better to vent your emotions than to allow them to become pent up, crushed and bitter!

The formula for a non-disastrous fighting and making up session is to make sure that it is always the last, not the first option available. Be forthright but objective in what you say – not spiteful or unkind – and bear in mind that the act of reconciliation must be completed soon afterwards, ideally the same day, but certainly not much longer. For that to happen a time-honoured scenario will need to be played out; one of you must hold out an olive branch to make up – definitely the harder of the two roles – and the other must have the decency to accept it gladly, graciously and unconditionally.

It would be trite and unconvincing of me to say that these two roles should be swapped in a civilised manner, by rotation, and shared equally throughout the life of the relationship because these things just don't pan out that way. They should, but in reality the outcome can be very different, very negative and sometimes terminal. When emotions are running high between two hot-blooded lovers, anything, including murder, can happen.

One thing is constant and can be relied on in times of upheaval and uncertainty. In all magnificent twosomes, there is a natural peacemaker-cum-maker-upper who shows him or herself more willing to end hostilities than the other. This person is quite often the stronger character mentally, the more loving partner and the more mature of the two. This has nothing to do with age.

Some couples say they never fight and this is commendable if there is no underlying friction, no issues that have been buried under the carpet for fear of disturbing the status quo. But, sceptical person that I am, I can't help wondering if everything is quite as kosher and rosy as we are led to believe, in these seemingly flawless relationships where neither party has a cross word to say to the other. My experience of human relationships in general and counselling in particular tells me not! Any couples who have been together for less than 20 years where both parties agree on everything, disagreeing on nothing, are not conducting a relationship that I recognise. One of them is kidding themselves and the other is being indulged.

Tatiana and I sometimes fight with a ferocity that frightens us both. Neither of us can sleep afterwards until we have made up. Sometimes, as a result, we will endure an entire night of misery, each of us too furious with the other to touch, but we won't go through two nights like that. We couldn't bear the pain – no matter what the original point of contention was or how it is resolved.

Although our fights become less and less frequent as our marriage matures, the very fact that we survive these storms of unmitigated hell makes us stronger and more secure as a couple. It's at times like this that the depth of our feelings and the power of our marriage is soundly tested, afterwards making us more appreciative and understanding of our love and need for each other; certain of our future together. If we simply enjoyed a life of perfect bliss with no problems and no differences of opinion, how could we be sure that the bond between us will withstand anything life throws at us?

Of course, we don't go looking for a fight and there would be no need to make up if we didn't let rip in the first place. There are far better ways to reconcile your differences by communicating with tenderness and clarity. But, on the down-to-earth premise that even the most angelic of women has her moments, and the coolest of men lose it periodically, now is the time to resolve to fight fair and to make up at the earliest opportunity. Conflict is never desirable, but if you intend to enjoy a passionate and meaningful relationship for the rest of the life be prepared! It's going to happen.

Once the trigger words have been unleashed, the vulnerable and touchy areas pinpointed and pressed, eyes have narrowed and locked, and the air has turned blue in the wrath of engagement, all hell is going to break loose until one of three things happens: a ceasefire is initiated; the combatants collapse from exhaustion; or one of them scores a verbal knockout!

Make-up must be swift and a solution to the underlying problem that caused you to fight must be found in the near future. The finest antidote for any lingering misgivings in the aftermath of battle is the loving hand of friendship, soothing and assuaging words that you'll find a way through this, a 'Forgive me' cuddle, and confirmation that you are still very much in love.

Reaffirmation that you care and a genuine demonstration of your love, affection and respect for your partner, despite everything, are of paramount importance at make or break times like this, because not only has your confidence in each other been shaken, but also conflicting messages have been being conveyed. According to a study conducted by the Eastman Kodak company in the USA, the words we speak make up only 7 per cent of the overall message we get across. Non-verbal communication such as smiles, stares, glares, frowns and gestures account for 55 per cent of the actual message received. The tone of voice we use to say what we have to say delivers the remaining 38 per cent of the message. This is because people don't assimilate every single word – it's too much hassle. They form a quick overview of what's being said by a combination of verbal and non-verbal clues.

In the event that you get the verbal equivalent of a kick in the teeth when you try to move things forward or hit an impenetrable wall of silence, consider, in the light of the information above, whether the non-verbal clues to your sincerity match the words you are using. Try another approach, perhaps, or endeavour to patch things up later when the atmosphere has cooled.

If you're trying to pacify the woman you have upset, don't labour heavily on solutions or invalidate her feelings, just concentrate on showing her that you are listening and that you care about her very much. If you're trying to get the man that you have hurt to re-engage with you and converse, remember that men, unlike most women, tend to clam up and go silent if they feel under intolerable pressure or overwhelmed by a problem. It's not that they are being deliberately awkward. It's just that they are probably shell-shocked and devastated by what's happened (even if they were wholly or partly to blame or – perish the thought – not responsible) and they usually need a little time and gentle coaxing before breaking their self-imposed firewall of silence.

Despite the fireworks that have gone before, you have to be able to relate to each other as lovers, best friends and partners again first, before you can begin to accurately identify the real source of the conflict, let alone solve it to the satisfaction of both parties.

Although few of us care to admit that we have a dark side, practicality dictates that if your partner can't accept the worst from you as well as the best, the two of you could experience a problem of incompatibility in the future. We can all strive and succeed in improving aspects of our behaviour and performance. What we can't do is completely change our personality, nor should we be urged or cajoled by our partners to do so.

This is why I don't believe in hiding things under the bed, or keeping feelings under the skin, for the sake of avoiding a disagreement. Even if the short-term payback of fighting and making up is a sleepless night, the long-term security of knowing that neither of us is afraid to confront the other when the need arises is worth any sacrifice.

The supposedly magic combination of love and the perfect partner is not enough to guarantee happiness and fulfilment for you both. You each need good communication and relationship skills to be able to relate to the other, particularly when problems arise. It is essential to be able to express your wants, your needs, your thoughts and even your innermost fears to each other with the expectation that you will be taken seriously.

Both of you deserve to feel understood, supported by the other and respected in your own right, but none of us is perfect. We all make mistakes and sometimes we will be selfish or neglectful. In the next chapter, you will find out how to communicate with tenderness and clarity so that there should be more negotiation and less fighting. Nevertheless, human nature dictates that we all have our moments – albeit, some more than others – so stand up for what you believe to be right, but never forget to kiss and make up without prompting and without hesitation. He or she who takes the initiative and assumes the role of peacemaker is the person I admire the most.

 The Bottom Line

Avoid confrontation when possible, but not at the expense of your self-respect or happiness.

CHAPTER 5

PART
5

Communicating with tenderness and clarity

Conversation has a kind of charm about it, an insinuating and insidious something that elicits secrets from us just like love or liqueur.

Seneca 4 BCE–CE 65

The thrust of this chapter is in the title. Hopefully, you will be enthused to adopt the habit of communicating with tenderness and clarity in all your day-to-day interactions and pillow talk with your partner, to enhance and secure the connection between you. Maybe you are one of those busy or laid-back people who are accustomed to skimming through the pages of books, rather than wresting every last word from them. If so, remember the title and in all your dealings with your partner from now on endeavour to combine tenderness and clarity with every word you utter. If you do that and nothing more, you will elevate your relationship and alleviate many of the problems of communication that couples encounter.

To reach the dizzy heights of magnificent twosomeness requires a willingness to try new ways of improving and energising your relationship. When you start communicating clearly, honestly and in a pleasant manner, every aspect of your relationship can develop and improve. It is never too late to do this and the straightforward tips and procedures here and in the next chapter are all you need to cut through the fog of misinterpretation and misunderstanding that has bedevilled communication between the sexes since words were invented.

In short, the essence of communicating with tenderness and clarity is contained within these three simple guidelines:

1 In a pleasant tone of voice and manner, express precisely what it is that you want to say.

2 Listen – not half listen – to what is being said without interruption.

3 After accepting that your partner's opinions and feelings may be different – but equally valid – from your own, respond openly, putting your own views forward, whether they are different or in accord.

It's obvious that we should all try to cut the complications out of life and say what we really mean because each of us is different. No one except you knows exactly what it is like to be you. Each of us inhabits our own individual world, much of it hidden from view. Other people can form an opinion of us based on what we look like, what we say and what we do. But if we give out false signals by saying what we don't mean, or by expressing what we do mean in such a disjointed or ramshackle way that we are not understood, is it surprising that even the most loving of partners is confused and sometimes responds inappropriately?

One of the most important and treasured aspects of my marriage to Tatiana is that we talk. We listen. We discuss. This might mean that we don't know what happens in *Coronation Street* or *EastEnders,* but we certainly know what's going down in each other's lives.

Communicating with tenderness and clarity means getting your message across in a nice, easy way. So many people say something other than what they actually mean. The listener becomes confused and gets the wrong idea about what is being said. The person speaking, instead of clarifying what has already been said, raises his or her voice and the shouting starts. The listener comes to the conclusion that they are being attacked or accused for some reason and all further communication, other than filthy looks, insults and deafening silences go straight out the window. Does this sound familiar?

Problems that get in the way of communicating with tenderness and clarity are:

- Using a negative or inappropriate manner and tone of voice
- Frowning, or looking angry or irritated when you speak
- Not saying what you really mean
- Taking forever to make your point
- Interrupting while your partner is still speaking
- Making false assumptions about what is being said based on your own feelings
- Not responding to what's being said
- Changing the subject
- Attempting to be a know-all
- Switching off, half listening or responding with empty gestures.

You will be surprised how quickly communication can be improved and how enjoyable chatting to your loved one will become, if you cut down on the conversation killers above and develop the conversation makers that follow.

Solutions that make communicating with tenderness and clarity easy and effective are:

- ✔ **Compliments!** In every magnificent twosome the world over both parties know how to pay their partner a genuine and much appreciated compliment. Do not let one single day go by without taking the trouble to pay your loved one a compliment that will make him or her glow inwardly with well-deserved pride and satisfaction.

- ✔ **Timing.** Good timing is essential to smooth and effective communication. Hitting your partner with a problem – real or imagined – the minute he or she gets home from a hard day's work is not on. Try giving prior thought to how and when you might raise difficult or delicate matters, and take the trouble to get your partner relaxed, sitting comfortably, perhaps with a drink, before proceeding. However, if the matter to be discussed is of an emotional nature, don't wait too long before bringing it up. It's essential to exercise control over your feelings rather than exploding with pent-up emotion because you waited for the perfect moment that didn't arrive.

- ✔ **Rationalising your thoughts.** If you were going to see a professional speaker at a life-enriching event, you know perfectly well that that speaker will have practised and prepared his or her speech so that it can be delivered with assurance and effect. Your partner is more important to you than all the delegates put together at the greatest event, so take a lead from the professionals and prepare your thoughts so that you can deliver what you have to say with tenderness and clarity. Surely you can invest 10 minutes of your journey home from work or 10 minutes of your lunch break to prepare what you are going to say in order to give your partner every opportunity to respond positively to you?

- ✔ **Understanding your feelings.** Planning a time to talk about delicate matters allows you to examine your feelings more calmly. Attacking your partner by saying something like, 'You were drooling all over my friend at the party last night,' might have more to do with a lack of security on your part than any interest your partner might have in your friend. Expressing what you really feel is an act of courage. When you are intimately involved in a relationship, it can be off-putting to admit your innermost feelings because you will be exposed and vulnerable. But if the relationship is a good one, there will be trust in each other and it is better to say what is on your mind than to leave your partner to guess.

The most effective means to affect a positive improvement in the way you communicate is to record or film yourself having a real or imagined conversation with your partner, then to listen to or watch the playback. Even if your first attempt leaves much to be desired, persevere for a few short days or weeks and you'll be amazed how much more concise, sincere and coherent you become with practice. This won't just enrich your personal life, it will also raise your game at work, in negotiations and in business. And think of the fun you'll have when you forget to destroy the evidence and your partner switches it on for you!

The Bottom Line

> Communicating with tenderness and clarity means getting your point across nice and easy.

CHAPTER 6

PART
5

Resolving problems, overcoming barriers

Once a woman has forgiven her man, she must not reheat his sins for breakfast.

Marlene Dietrich 1901– 92
(And the same applies to men)

In the last chapter, I describe how Tatiana and I talk over our evening meal. If we have a problem, or a potential problem, this is often where it will come out. We are happy about this; there is no awkwardness, no hostility, just a confidence that we can deal with the problem and end up on the same side. This is our system. With, perhaps, only the occasional hitch, it works well for us.

However, every couple is different and our system is not necessarily the ideal model for everyone. It is up to each pair to develop their own way, one that suits their respective temperaments and works for them. It may be that they talk frequently or leave it until they think the air needs to be cleared! In any event, to reach magnificent twosomeness there is a definite need for a system for resolving problems and overcoming barriers, otherwise the partnership is going to be soured.

If you're feeling brave and the two of you regularly experience difficulties of one kind or another, you might consider my favourite problem-solving system, which has proved highly effective for many couples, some of whom, despite being very much in love, would probably have ended up tearing their relationship apart.

This enjoyable method of communicating with tenderness and clarity by special appointment, once a week, will spare you a quagmire of potential upsets. This procedure is so powerful it can resurrect a relationship that's heading due south, or save a hitherto shaky marriage that would otherwise be blown apart by a minefield of unresolved problems and seemingly insurmountable obstacles.

The fundamental cause of problems and barriers between the sexes is simple enough: men and women are different!

Men often have a problem discussing feelings and we do not like it when we are cornered, snared or unexpectedly hit with a problem, particularly when we come up with an ingenious and immediate solution only to find that that is not what is required of us!

Women usually have no problem communicating with tenderness (well, providing they haven't been upset), but communicating with clarity, as opposed to going round the houses and dodging from one subject to another along the way, can sometimes be an area that is ripe for development. Men are not telepathic. Perhaps we should know what is the matter without being told, but frequently we don't.

Also, we don't react well to being dropped little clues or hints about gathering storm clouds or developing dramas. We need to be told what is the matter with candour and accuracy. Timing is of the essence. Whereas women are more flexible and impulsive in

RESOLVING PROBLEMS, OVERCOMING BARRIERS

speech, men sometimes need time to prepare themselves for close encounters of the verbal kind.

To accommodate the contrasting approaches to communication by men and women, we are going to set in motion a chain of events that will go a long way to filter out aggravation from your relationship. I want you to set up a regular weekly date with your partner – same time, same day, place variable – although, I accept that if your working life is complicated by shift patterns or you live a long way apart, you may have to build flexibility into this routine. It doesn't matter whether it's a regular dinner date, a lunch date or a get-together in a motorway cafeteria. The important thing is that it happens. Arrive in the mood to settle all differences and to move the relationship onwards and upwards.

Make a point of:

- Laughing at any fiascos or foul-ups – however caused and regardless of who was to blame – in the week that has been and gone.

- Creating a relaxed and positive environment in which to decide how things could be better managed in future.

- Putting on the table for discussion – each partner in turn – any concerns that have been stripping the gloss from the relationship in the previous week.

- Reconfirming in both words and deeds that you are both batting on the same side and striving for a better future together. At entry level this might consist of a tender touch and an admission (if appropriate) that one of you was wrong, hasty or thoughtless, accompanied by the words 'I'm sorry.'

- Enjoying yourself and the company of the person you love in an environment that is both productive and non-threatening. Don't concern yourselves with any hustle and bustle going on around you. This is your life and this is the time of the week when you iron out any wrinkles.

- Understanding that this weekly date is special, takes priority over everything else and may only be rescheduled by prior agreement in the most urgent and pressing of circumstances.

If irreconcilable differences remain despite your best efforts to sort things out, the problem will invariably centre upon one partner's beliefs and sense of values, or the feeling that their identity is being threatened in some way. People can get very stuck and entrenched when they feel any violation of these core elements has occurred. The key to progress when major blocks of this nature remain is to admit candidly – as friends and lovers, not combatants – that you haven't found a means of resolution *yet*. The addition of this one optimistic and powerful word emphasises the likelihood of a successful outcome.

The Bottom Line

Aim to develop a win/win strategy that suits you both.

Togetherness – friendship and trust

Richard: 'I have no idea where Judy and I will be in three, even two years from now: all our futures lie below the horizon. But as long as, wherever it is, we're together, we'll be okay.'
Judy: 'As long as I have my family, my health and Richard, I count myself a lucky woman.'

Richard Madeley and Judy Finnigan

These are fundamental building blocks. If this is to be a union that will soar, magnetise the two of you and deliver happiness and a sense of togetherness beyond anything you have ever experienced, each of you must warrant the other's friendship and trust. You both must prove to be loyal and trustworthy friends because great relationships are made from stuff like this. It is the essence of magnificent twosomeness!

Decades from now – right up to the actual the moment you die – your investment in a lasting and trust-honouring friendship with each other will still be paying dividends in terms of satisfaction, security and peace of mind. That investment, which no amount of money can buy, accumulates in value through you being there for your partner. It can keep love alive and deliver a special kind of closeness that no one can prise apart.

A revealing way to establish where you are in your life at the moment and whether you have what it takes to offer real friendship and to justify your partner's trust, is to ask yourself what is it that you want from your relationship. Do you want something along the lines of the past, or have you set your heart upon doing whatever it takes (including making the sacrifices) to build a relationship that never comes off the rails?

If the prospect of one-night stands and the excitement of the unpredictable still makes your pulse race, you could be found wanting. Imagine projecting your life five years forward. Would you like it to be as it was in the past, or would you prefer to be forging ahead with a rewarding and ever-developing relationship founded not only on love, but also in the warmth of friendship and in the comfort and security of trust?

What can you do to nurture friendship and trust in your relationship, regardless of how good or fragile it is now? Here are a few suggestions that everyone who is serious about making it to magnificent twosomeness can use to lay firm tracks to a lasting future together.

Ways to deepen friendship and trust with your lover and partner
- Give a sincere and meaningful welcome the next time you set eyes on each other.

- Spend more time together.

- Demonstrate that you can be trusted by keeping your word when you give it. If you say you are going to do something, do it! If you say you're not going to do something, don't!

- Show your appreciation when something is done for you.

- Make life more exciting for you both by doing different things.

- Ensure that there is reasonable parity in chores.

- Have fun and derive the maximum pleasure from the everyday things you do together.

- Support and comfort each other when things are difficult.

- Demonstrate that you can be unselfish and caring by anticipating needs.

- Listen to what is said.

- Adopt a problem-solving procedure that suits you both.

- Show your generosity with a surprise or an unexpected gift.

- Get actively involved in doing more things together – things that you both want to do.

- Try to be unfazed and see the funny side of things, even if one of you should collide with the other's car. Your concern in these circumstances should be that you are both okay.

- Have each other's best interests at heart.

- Be kind.

I know it isn't easy in this high-pressure age of conflicting demands and overlapping pressures on your time, but if you set aside quality time for each other you will achieve very positive things in the relationship. First, you give a clear and highly significant message that you are important and very special to each other. Second, the more time you spend together, the more you tune in to each other's ways of doing things, the more you see the world through each other's eyes, the greater the bond between you.

 The Bottom Line

Friendship and trust are the ultimate investment for lovers and partners to make in each other.

Tolerance and understanding

The course of true love never did run smooth.

William Shakespeare 1564–1616

Tolerance and understanding are two unfashionable qualities that are seldom appreciated until you get into trouble and find yourself yearning for them. You could be happily married and devoted to each other, but if one partner feels an overwhelming desire to train to run a marathon, write a book or start a business, tolerance and understanding will be required.

I view these qualities as the soothing balm that makes things better when the relationship is under strain. They facilitate the ability to respond with open-mindedness and empathy when plans change, new opportunities present themselves, or things go wrong. It also means giving up the right to be right all the time. When you insist on being right, what you communicate to your partner is that he or she is wrong. Agreeing to differ is better. Sometimes, when we are sure we are right, we find that a new fact, a previously undisclosed piece of information, can change our view.

Some things are black and white, of course, but in relationships that stand the test of time, both parties realise that there can be many shades and interpretations of right, depending on your belief structure, your upbringing and how you look at the situation. Better to avoid fighting with your loved one for the sake of winning when, if you really are going for magnificent twosomeness, you both have so much going for you.

The Bottom Line

Tolerance and understanding are the soothing balm that eases the pain.

CHAPTER 9

PART
5

Respect

How I did respect you when you dared to speak the truth to me!

Anthony Trollope 1815–82

All the love in the world will not be enough for you and your partner to make it to magnificent twosomeness if you lack genuine respect for each other. To be able to weather the storms of life, to create the impetus for an ever-developing relationship and to have the capacity to go on indefinitely making each other happy and satisfied, respect is essential. Without it, your relationship will collapse, or worse still – slowly stagnate.

Some couples start off with a healthy measure of respect for each other and this respect grows, as it should do, through merit and with the passage of time, along with their love. But, as they share more and greater aspects of their lives – becoming increasingly intimate, familiar and comfortable – the expression of respect goes.

Little things like 'please' and 'thank you' disappear from the everyday vocabulary. Interrupting, or cutting their partner off in mid-sentence, becomes commonplace, and dismissive gestures like rolling one's eyes back in disdain and ridiculing the other in public further erode the foundations of the relationship. The person on the receiving end of this lack of respect – which may not be intentional – should immediately pull up the offending partner and demand the respect they are entitled to. But, often, they don't! They simply become disillusioned and drift into the same unfortunate pattern of behaviour as their 'taking you for granted' partner. Over time, the partners, who may well love each other, demonstrate less and less respect, the downhill slide gathers momentum and the relationship hits the buffers.

One of the lessons I have learned from Afro-Caribbean people is the importance of respect in their cultures. The word crops up frequently in conversation whether it's parents dealing with their children, adults in discussion with each other or young people speaking to their contemporaries, even in the context of arguments that could develop into something more physical. It is necessary to show respect where it is due and a major failing not to show it.

Many of us pride ourselves on our courtesy. We are scrupulous with our manners and modes of behaviour with strangers. We hold open doors for them, we give them directions when called upon and render assistance when needed. With friends and colleagues we often listen to their opinions without interruption, we seldom use a contemptuous tone when they come up with something completely stupid and we don't collapse laughing at their dress-sense, facial adornments or hairstyles. So, why is that we treat friends and strangers alike with charm and respect, but when we go home to greet the love of our life, we take this wonderful person for granted, slam doors, act abruptly and are sometimes downright rude? Why can't we treat this special VIP as well as – if not better than – the people we don't love?

You've heard the cliché 'familiarity breeds contempt'. Well, it's true! One of the things that long-term lovers, lifelong partners and happily married couples have in common is the ability to admire and hold their partner in high esteem, no matter how familiar they become. Of course, we all have moments when we make absolute fools of ourselves and respect goes flying out the window, but in any well-grounded, robust and lasting relationship, the absence of respect is a very temporary phenomenon.

One of the first visible signs of a relationship that is heading for trouble is when people take advantage of the privileged position of love and intimacy they share with their partner to treat each other with contempt and sarcasm. The lack of respect they have for each other is painfully clear for all to see. Very soon, their love will be dead and gone. Like many things in life, a line must not be crossed. It's fine to laugh, joke and good-humouredly poke fun at each other when you are alone together. It's not okay to be dismissive, sarcastic or disrespectful.

Classic respect killers include:

- Failing to be polite and attentive
- Forgetting or failing to display good manners by saying 'please' and 'thank you'
- Mocking or belittling your partner
- Interrupting, rather than allowing the other person to finish what they have to say
- Walking out of the room while your partner is still speaking
- Taking your loved one for granted
- Revealing negative things about your partner in public
- Failing to respect each other's vulnerabilities
- Neglecting to edit yourself when you speak in a harsh, cold or contentious tone of voice
- Not bothering to treat your partner with the love and consideration that he or she deserves

- Failure to keep your word or honour your commitments

- Drunken, irresponsible, lewd or violent behaviour

- Driving at a speed and distance from the vehicle in front that is uncomfortable for your partner, when he or she is in the passenger seat.

Relationships grow strong and lasting when people feel valued, loved and appreciated. Love may well be the driving force behind this growth and longevity, but care and consideration, together with courtesy and good manners – in a word, respect – are both the safety and the navigation systems that keep love alive and heading in the right direction. Most of all, respect is about making your partner feel treasured, deeply loved and wanted; it is confirmation that he or she was right to fall in love with you. You get respect by giving it!

 The Bottom Line

> The greatest gift a man or a woman can give to their partner is to treat them with respect.

CHAPTER 10

PART
5

Commitment

When I fall in love, it will be forever.

sung by Nat King Cole 1917–65

Contrary to a widely held view put forward in relationship books, men are no less willing to commit to a lasting relationship than women are. They simply arrive at the commitment stage through a meandering and somewhat bizarre thought process that can take a little time to come together.

In what is increasingly becoming a woman's world, men often need extra time to evaluate their position and to satisfy themselves that their partner's love is genuine and they are not being set up for a helter-skelter ride with a kiss at the front-end and a shafting down the line. You can't blame us for being wary, with the scary divorce rates in the west and the perceived bias in the law courts in favour of women that almost guarantees that men will feel resentful at the loss of their home, kids and a proportion of their future earnings.

It is essential to get this commitment thing sorted, because non-existent or lukewarm commitment to or from your partner is toxic and the underlying root cause of virtually every relationship collapse, regardless of whether short or long term. If you are over 30 and you live with your partner or you see each other a lot, you should know for sure within six or 12 months if your partner is the one for you. No ifs, no buts, no I'm not sure! This applies equally to men and women, because without commitment your relationship will drift.

The decision to commit to Mr or Ms Absolutely Right, and vice versa, will invigorate and liberate you emotionally, socially, economically and practically. You will be pulling meaningfully and purposefully in the same direction with your combined energy, attention and renewed focus. Everything becomes possible. Fears of freedom lost evaporate as you become aware of a greater freedom gained; freedom from uncertainty, indecision and being alone and unloved. A whole new world of ecstasy opens for you to explore and enjoy together. If the two of you are moving forward hand in hand on this one, well done!

And, if you haven't got it sorted yet?

You will need to work towards some sort of mutual understanding on commitment, because otherwise you might find out in future years that what you hoped was the basis for a permanent relationship is grounded in commitment phobia, insecurity or sheer convenience, not bedrock.

There is no point in persuading your partner to do something against his or her will, or extracting a promise of future engagement from someone who is running scared. But there is much to be gained, when the time is right, from finding out with absolute clarity and clear cut resolution, what the problem with commitment is and whether it can be overcome.

You would be amazed how many different reasons there are why men, who are besotted with their partner, won't commit, and you may never find out what your guy's problem is unless you gently probe and establish the truth. A man may genuinely believe that his prospects are not good enough to keep you, that he doesn't have enough money to make you happy or that he doesn't really deserve such a wonderful woman as you.

Be warned, emotional shutdown and the big freeze await any woman who is clumsy in her attempts to cajole her man into confronting his demons. Women, also, have irrational reasons that feed their own insecurities and fears. However, they are usually more willing to talk about them.

If you are the only person in your relationship who is prepared to commit and go the distance, but it's magnificent twosomeness you've set your heart on, you need to dump your partner, and find someone who's there for you every step of the way. But first, before you consider taking such decisive action, let us see if we can tease out the problem and solve it.

Unless your partner is a serial or incurable commitment-phobe, reluctance to commit usually boils down to one of three fears. The first is a fear of being proved right, a fear of the future, some of which I have already signalled in previous paragraphs.

The best way to flush out such fears is to mitigate your partner's anxieties by admitting to insecurities of your own and to show yourself receptive to your partner's support and guidance in this area. In the process of being comforted, reassured and told what to do, gradually turn the whole thing around into a relaxed and liberating general confession session.

Another similar and more rational explanation that fits into this category is a very real fear your partner may have that he or she wouldn't be able to live up to their long-term commitments to you, even though they might wish to. As such, they are reluctant to commit because they foresee a possibility that they might let you down. But there are limits to all this. None of us can foretell the future. We can never be certain of success; we can only do our absolute best to make things work out the way we want.

The second fear that can immobilise an otherwise intelligent and forward-looking person from fully committing to their loved one is the fear of being hurt. Many people who have been divorced or gone through the trauma of a major break-up, particularly after a long-term relationship where children are involved, are afraid that history will repeat itself and they might end up getting more of what they got before. They will need plenty of reassurance and a softly-softly approach.

The third fear that can nag men and women alike when the time comes to commit, split, or accept the status quo, is the fear of losing their freedom. This final staging-post of dread and self-doubt before change of one type or another is inevitable, can have three horns on its head and they are often shaped something like this.

1 **I won't be able to do what I want, when I want, how I want!** No, not all the time, because every successful relationship involves a generous measure of give and take, as well as sufficient room to manoeuvre to allow both parties to realise their personal dreams and ambitions, in addition to exploring deeper levels of love, intimacy and fulfilment together.

2 **Horror of horrors – we might end up like my parents or the potential in-laws!** Some kids are lucky enough to have the most loving and wonderful parents who make valuable role models, but for those of us who missed out, it's only to be expected that we inherited a dysfunctional view of getting older together.

3 **What if someone better comes along? I'll be trapped.** Frankly, if you are simply marking time with your partner, insecure or using the person who loves you as bait, I think you might have missed the point of this book. Have the decency to tell your partner that it's over, and make a genuine attempt to find the right partner, someone that you can actually admire, love and cherish; someone who you would continue to want even if half-a-dozen Miss World or Mr Universe contestants threw themselves naked at your feet. If you think I'm joking, think again. You, like me some way back in the past, may have a long way to go before you discover true happiness and fulfilment with a future partner, but don't give up.

Real commitment grows and develops with shared experiences. Your ideas about the future are important: announcing to family and friends that you are an item, renting a flat together, or popping the question and (assuming you get a 'Yes') planning the wedding. Issues like this have to be tackled and hopefully agreed so that the way forward can be decided.

Once you get together as a committed twosome and begin planning the future, then at some point you will experience a dramatic inner shift. Let's call this burning commitment. This brings with it the power to achieve the seemingly impossible. It carries with it an unstoppable momentum; an unshakeable determination to make it to magnificent twosomeness whereby the love you feel for each other grows and grows because you know you are there for each other.

Burning commitment is deciding that you're going to make the relationship work, no matter what. You're the one who's going to take the lead, build the foundations for a lasting relationship, propel the relationship forward and assume the responsibility to show how great relationships are created. No matter if you've never succeeded in a long-term relationship before, never mind if you have failed to achieve gold in anything you've ever attempted, with burning commitment in your heart, as well as love, you and your partner are heading for happiness and fulfilment.

But it takes two, doesn't it?

Yes, that's right, but in any healthy relationship where one partner is looking out for the other, being there for them, listening to their dreams, fuelling their ambitions and loving them without preconditions, something stirs and awakens within the partner receiving love like this and they reciprocate in kind.

The Bottom Line

The moment you definitely commit, your life changes gear and your relationship is enriched.

PART 6

The Matchmaking Equation

$$\sum_{n=1}^{20} (X_n + Y_n)^2 = (X_1 + Y_1)^2 + (X_2 + Y_2)^2 + \ldots + (X_{20} + Y_{20})^2 = 100$$

'Eureka! I have found it.'

Archimedes 287–212 BCE

This can't be reduced to maths – can it?

$$\sum_{n=1}^{20} (X_n + Y_n)^2 = (X_1 + Y_1)^2 + (X_2 + Y_2)^2 + \ldots + (X_{20} + Y_{20})^2 = 100$$

You can't be serious! Well, yes! This is Tatiana speaking. I was introduced to you as David's wife and co-author in the foreword to the book and you haven't heard a peep from me since. I shall be taking you through this part of the book.

I want to show you how choosing the right partner is underpinned by mathematics. Most things are: the motion of the planets, the quality of the signal on your mobile phone, how your car runs; and your love life is no exception. Stick with me on this one, even if the prospect of crunching numbers is not your idea of fun.

The good news is that I have done most of the work and all of the complicated calculations for you. It doesn't matter whether or not you understand the equation or how it works. The important thing to know is that it does work. For the benefit of all you mathematicians out there, I will of course explain the formula. But at this point all you need to know is that it works and applies directly to you and your partner.

Give me an hour or so of your undivided attention now and I will help you to find out if your current partner is the one for you. Here, over the next four chapters, you have a unique opportunity to find out if the two of you have what it takes to make each other happy in 10, 20, 30 years from now, not just for the short-term. What's more, in the event that your relationship is destined to prove short-lived, you can find this out quickly, saving yourself months or even years marking time with the wrong person.

In Chapters 2 and 3 of this section, I am going to present you and your partner with separate questionnaires. In order to input all the necessary personal information to make the equation relevant to you, three different levels of your relationship will be evaluated. These tests will be scored and assessed to produce an all-embracing calculation of your long-term compatibility and likelihood of happiness formulated from 20 crucial factors ranging from chemistry to commitment.

In an ideal scenario, you will complete this exercise alone when your partner is not by your side, and your partner will complete the same exercise with no input from you and no knowledge whatsoever of your answers. However, in my experience, the ideal conditions do not always present themselves when required, so I'm going to give you a fallback position for completing and scoring both sets of questionnaires if only one partner to the relationship is available or willing to get involved.

This fallback position is only viable, of course, if you believe you know yourself and your partner well enough to respond to all questions with accuracy and candour. Don't kid yourself with phoney answers because by doing so, you blind yourself to the truth, you rob yourself of the opportunity of seeing through the fog of love and finding out if your partner really is Mr or Ms Absolutely Right.

If you don't want to get involved in the mathematics of the matchmaking equation, skip the rest of this chapter. For the mathematically inquisitive, read on!

The essence of the equation is that each partner brings certain factors into a relationship. These factors are combined when two people get together in a personal relationship or marriage and empowered in the equation by a mathematical operation called 'squaring'. This has the effect of fast forwarding the consequences of uniting these combined factors by multiplication and indicating whether the parties to the relationship are suited in the long term or not. In mathematical terms, this can be stated as follows, with 100 representing the ideal match:

$$\sum_{n=1}^{20} (X_n + Y_n)^2 = (X_1 + Y_1)^2 + (X_2 + Y_2)^2 + \ldots + (X_{20} + Y_{20})^2 = 100$$

Basic keys and gender note:
X_1 – the first variable characteristic of the first person
Y_1 – the first variable characteristic of the partner
$(X_1 + Y_1)^2$ – the multiplied effect of these characteristics on the parties to a relationship
X_2, Y_2, rising consecutively to X_{20}, Y_{20} – the other characteristics of the partners
$\sum_{n=1}^{n} (X_n + Y_n)^2$ – the cumulative effect of all the characteristics of both partners

Incidentally, in terms of human genetics, the X-chromosome denotes the female sex and the Y-chromosome denotes the male of the species, but for the purposes of the equation, X can be Y and Y can be X because the matchmaking equation is equally valid for same-sex relationships.

The Matchmaking Equation was formulated and quantified by isolating the building blocks and decisive factors in lasting relationships to be found in happy and mature marriages. The equation has three distinct sets of dynamics to it, which David and I refer to as tiers. The first tier of your relationship to evaluate, with a maximum potential score equal to 36 per cent of the total equation, involves the primary building blocks to any loving relationship: lust, friendship, trust and respect.

These aspects of love are regarded as essential if your relationship is to grow and become permanent. You and your partner's strength in these areas will be tested. The optimum score, per building block, for each couple, is three points (one point between the partners per question providing both parties answer correctly). If only one partner answers correctly the score for that question is zero.

Next, the score for each building block (each set of three questions) is added together to arrive at a subtotal. Then the subtotal is squared by multiplying the figure by itself. For instance, assuming a couple scored the maximum number of points possible – three – for each of the four building blocks, then, they would square three and arrive at nine. Finally, they would multiply nine by the number of building blocks – four – successfully completing the first tier of the equation with 36 points (36 per cent of the total equation). This test is valid for any couple who have been going out together on a regular basis for at least three months.

The second tier centres upon compatibility and accounts for 44 per cent of the value of the equation. It is ideal for couples who have been together for more than six months.

The partners will need to demonstrate that they have no fewer than 11 different elements of compatibility to score maximum points. Indicating the extent to which they agree or disagree with a series of one line statements and circling the appropriate symbol on the reference key will test this. The parties to the relationship should complete separate questionnaires with no discussion and no access to each other's responses during the process.

The points scored for each of the 11 elements of compatibility are then added together, squared and totalled in the same manner as for tier one.

Now to the synthesis, the third and final tier of the equation, which takes into account the advanced building blocks to a secure and lasting relationship: equilibrium, tolerance, understanding, togetherness and commitment. In total, the questions on synthesis carry a potential score worth 20 per cent of the equation, and the test presupposes that the parties to the relationship have been seriously dating for at least 12 months.

This test consists of five sections and one point per couple is scored when both parties select an option that scores – even when the responses chosen from the option list differ between participants. Naturally, no score is recorded when either or both parties choose a non-scoring answer.

The total points (maximum two per section) are added together for each section and then squared in the same way as for tiers 1 and 2. For example, if you scored maximum points in every section (2 × 5), squaring the result from each section will produce 4 × 5 and a combined score of 20 to complete the third and final tier of the equation. Providing that optimum scores had been recorded during both the first and the second tiers, the equation is complete and you and you partner are destined for magnificent twosomeness with an awesome score of 100.

A simplified set of scoring instructions appears later so that everyone can accurately review their results after completing the questionnaire. The higher the score, the more likely it is that you are right for each other.

The Bottom Line

> Maximise your chances of seeing clearly through the fog of love: answer the questions honestly.

Essentials –
the recipe for
lasting love

$$\sum_{n=1}^{20} (X_n + Y_n)^2 = (X_1 + Y_1)^2 + (X_2 + Y_2)^2 + \ldots + (X_{20} + Y_{20})^2 = 100$$

The concept of a recipe for lasting love might at first take your breath away, but there is one and each of the vital ingredients – all 20 of them – we have explored in the book already and we will test in the equation.

The purpose of the questionnaire that follows is to find out if the relationship you have chosen has the potential to be an ideal match and whether or not you have what it takes to make each other happy and fulfilled in the future.

Only you, or you and your partner, need ever know the results so you can relax and be absolutely forthright and truthful with your answers to the questionnaire. If you are going to do this alone, without your partner's involvement, which is far from ideal, but can be beneficial in helping you to assess your relationship, you will need to fill in both your questionnaire, which appears here, and afterwards the one for your partner. Do not attempt to fill in both at the same time.

Let's get started! The rest of this chapter consists of three separate tests, each dealing with a different aspect of your relationship. Simply answer the questions and respond to the statements by filling in the questionnaire. A duplicate appears in the next chapter for your partner to fill in separately. Detach it or, if you don't want to deface or damage the book, copy it and give it to your partner for completion. Whatever you do, don't discuss the contents of the questionnaires or show each other your answers until you have both completed them.

TIER ONE: The primary building blocks to a secure and lasting relationship: lust, friendship, trust and respect.
Answer yes or no to the questions by ticking the appropriate box.

Yes No

Lust

1 Can you think of three things that really turn you on about your partner? ☐☐

2 If you had the option to trade in your partner for someone younger, more handsome, or beautiful, would you do it? ☐☐

3 Does your partner touch or kiss you affectionately? ☐☐

Friendship

4 Outside the bedroom, do you enjoy spending time simply being with your partner? ☐☐

Yes No

5 Can you be playful, relaxed and even
outrageous at times with your partner,
without upsetting or offending him or her?

6 Is there someone in your network of friends
who you regard as a closer friend than your
partner?

Trust

7 Does your partner always turn up when
they say they will?

8 If there was a problem that you needed help
with urgently, would it be your partner you
would turn to?

9 Can you be sure that you will make up with
your partner after a row?

Respect

10 Can you think of three reasons why you
respect your partner?

11 Does your partner usually own up to their
own mistakes when things go wrong?

12 Do you support your partner in their
aspirations for the future?

TIER TWO: The decisive areas of compatibility.

This section looks at how much you and your partner have in
common, and gauges how the two of you are likely to get on in the
future when the early flushes of love have either evaporated or
metamorphosed into lasting devotion. It explores 11 major areas
of compatibility (or potential friction) and can be instrumental in

forecasting the long-term potential of your relationship, even if you have only been together for a few short months or years.

Areas of particular interest in this test include communication/ interaction, emotional expression, upbringing, education/ interpersonal skills, religious/political/personal views, ambition/ needs/children, sex drive/fidelity, work/financial security, shared interests, lifestyle, relaxation and leisure.

All you have to do is indicate the extent to which you agree or disagree with each statement that follows by circling the appropriate response. You must not circle more than one response. You will invalidate the questionnaire if you allow your partner to see your answers before they have completed theirs.

AA = Absolutely agree, A = Agree, N = Neutral/not applicable, D = Disagree,
DD = Definitely disagree

Communication/interaction

13 I feel good when I'm with my partner.   AA A N D DD

14 We enjoy talking with each other.   AA A N D DD

15 My partner makes me laugh.   AA A N D DD

16 I get on well when I am meeting
   my partner's family and friends.   AA A N D DD

Emotional expression

17 I believe that we bring out the best in   AA A N D DD
   each other.

18 If my partner accidentally crashed   AA A N D DD
   my car, I would be okay about it.

19 I sometimes feel intimidated by   AA A N D DD
   my partner.

20 I have considered the possible long-term implications and I am relaxed and comfortable about the age difference between us.　　AA A N D DD

Upbringing

21 My partner's approach to life may be different from mine, but I like it that way.　　AA A N D DD

22 My partner is from the same ethnic origin and cultural background.　　AA A N D DD

23 I believe in decency and fair play.　　AA A N D DD

24 Status is important to me.　　AA A N D DD

Education/interpersonal skills

25 I am usually relaxed and comfortable in my partner's company.　　AA A N D DD

26 I regard myself as well educated.　　AA A N D DD

27 I believe I have higher than average intelligence.　　AA A N D DD

28 My problem-solving skills are good.　　AA A N D DD

Religious/political/personal views/habits

29 I have strong political views.　　AA A N D DD

30 I have strong religious/ anti-religious views.　　AA A N D DD

31 I can't stand people smoking around me.　　AA A N D DD

32 I take recreational drugs.   AA A N D DD

Ambition/needs/children

33 I believe we are making progress   AA A N D DD
    in anticipating each other's needs.

34 We have shared ambitions for   AA A N D DD
    the future.

35 I find the relationship stimulating   AA A N D DD
    and fulfilling.

36 I would like to have children/   AA A N D DD
    more children.

Sex drive/fidelity

37 My sex drive is insatiable,   AA A N D DD
    I am always up for it.

38 Our sex life is good.   AA A N D DD

39 Regular sex is not a requirement   AA A N D DD
    for me.

40 Sexual fidelity is extremely important   AA A N D DD
    to me.

Work/financial security

41 I value happiness and satisfaction   AA A N D DD
    more highly than money.

42 Financial security is very important   AA A N D DD
    to me.

43 I believe in self-development and   AA A N D DD
    making life better.

44 I enjoy my work/occupation/business/   AA A N D DD
full-time parenting/retirement.

Shared interests

45 I can think of six or more non-sexual   AA A N D DD
activities we enjoy together.

46 We love going out regularly together.   AA A N D DD

47 We share similar values across a range   AA A N D DD
of topics.

48 Family life is very important to me.   AA A N D DD

Lifestyle

49 I am adventurous in my choice of   AA A N D DD
restaurants when eating out.

50 I like to eat chips with most of my   AA A N D DD
hot meals.

51 I like classical music.   AA A N D DD

52 My lifestyle includes good books,   AA A N D DD
films, theatre.

Relaxation and leisure

53 I watch TV for a couple of hours or   AA A N D DD
more several nights each week.

54 I enjoy a few drinks most nights.   AA A N D DD

55 I can't stand football.   AA A N D DD

56 I am willing to accept my partner's   AA A N D DD
choice of holiday destination even
if it doesn't appeal to me.

TIER THREE: The advanced building blocks to a secure and lasting relationship: equilibrium, tolerance, understanding, togetherness and commitment.

Circle the response (only one per question) that seems most appropriate to you and your relationship.

Equilibrium

57 Let's say you had a right royal ding-dong! You've argued, got uptight, let off a lot off steam and the two of you are mad at each other. Afterwards, when you've made up, talked things through rationally, listened to each other's viewpoints and come up with a solution that suits you both, do you feel even closer than you were before?

    a Always
    b Often
    c Seldom
    d Never
    e Not applicable – we don't argue

58 Who's getting the best deal out of the relationship?

    a Me
    b My partner
    c Both of us
    d It's fairly equal
    e Don't know

Tolerance

59 When your partner is under pressure or stress, are you (or do you think you will be) able to accept him/her at

their worst? (The question assumes that 'their worst' does not include violence of any kind.)

a Yes
b No
c Maybe

60 Your partner is doing their best, but making a right hash of some trivial task that you could do far better. Do you:

a Point out the error of their ways?
b Criticise?
c Offer to help?
d Lie back and enjoy the unfolding fiasco?
e Get stuck in and do-it-yourself?

Understanding

61 Do you find it easy to confide in your partner?

a Yes
b No
c Occasionally
d Most of the time

62 In all probability, you and your partner have some needs, habits, traits, or desires that are not wholly compatible. Do you:

a Regard yourselves as perfect in every way?
b Try to get your partner to change to suit you?
c Change to suit your partner?
d Work together to bring about a gradual merging of compatibility?
e Put your partner's needs before your own occasionally?

Togetherness

63 Looking ahead five years, is there room for your partner in your plans and aspirations?

    a Probably, but I can't be sure because I don't know what the future holds
    b I don't have any plans or aspirations for the future
    c Yes
    d Maybe
    e If all goes according to plan
    f I sincerely hope so

64 Do you share a common view of the relationship, but retain some independence?

    a Yes
    b No
    c Most of the time

Commitment

65 Can you think of anyone that you would rather spend your life with than your partner?

    a Yes
    b No
    c Yes, but this person is not available
    d Don't know
    e I'm not sure

66 If your partner was to fall from grace, would you stand squarely alongside him/her?

a I believe I would
b Except in extreme or unreasonable circumstances, I believe I would
c Probably
e Maybe
f Yes
g Yes, providing my partner hadn't been disloyal to me or acted indecently to anyone else
h No
i This decision must ultimately depend on the reaction of my family, friends, peer group, etc.

Well done! You now have exactly half of the information you will need to find out where your relationship fits in the Matchmaking Equation. Your partner's questionnaire, which is identical to yours, is itching to be filled out in the next chapter.

 The Bottom Line

Copy or detach the blank questionnaire on pages 248–58 and give it to your partner.

It takes two – your partner's contribution to the equation

$$\sum_{n=1}^{20} (X_n + Y_n)^2 = (X_1 + Y_1)^2 + (X_2 + Y_2)^2 + \ldots + (X_{20} + Y_{20})^2 = 100$$

Hello! My name's Tatiana and if your partner has unexpectedly presented you with this three-part questionnaire on relationships to fill in, I understand and fully sympathise with you if you're feeling surprised and taken aback. Don't worry, this questionnaire is an integral part of a book called *Countdown to Love*, and it really can help you and your partner to get the best out of your relationship. Everything in the questionnaire is completely confidential and only you and your partner need ever see it. The exciting bit comes later when you score and find out where you both fit in the Matchmaking Equation.

The premise behind the part of the book that your partner has just been reading is that successful relationships are underpinned by mathematics. Most things are – the motion of the planets, the quality of the signal on your mobile phone, how your car runs – and your love life is no exception.

The good news is that I have done most of the work and all of the complicated calculations for you. It doesn't matter whether or not you understand the equation on page 248 or how it works. The important thing to know is that it does work. Should you be a mathematician or someone who likes to know how things work, the formula is of course explained on pages 234–6. Your concern is to find out how you and your partner shape up as a pair towards a happy future.

TIER ONE: The primary building blocks to a secure and lasting relationship: lust, friendship, trust and respect.
Answer yes or no to the questions by ticking the appropriate box.

	Yes	No

Lust

1 Can you think of three things that really turn you on about your partner? ☐ ☐

2 If you had the option to trade in your partner for someone younger, more handsome, or beautiful, would you do it? ☐ ☐

3 Does your partner touch or kiss you affectionately? ☐ ☐

Friendship

4 Outside the bedroom, do you enjoy spending time simply being with your partner? ☐ ☐

Yes No

5 Can you be playful, relaxed and even outrageous at times with your partner, without upsetting or offending him or her? ☐☐

6 Is there someone in your network of friends who you regard as a closer friend than your partner? ☐☐

Trust

7 Does your partner always turn up when they say they will? ☐☐

8 If there was a problem that you needed help with urgently, would it be your partner you would turn to? ☐☐

9 Can you be sure that you will make up with your partner after a row? ☐☐

Respect

10 Can you think of three reasons why you respect your partner? ☐☐

11 Does your partner usually own up to their own mistakes when things go wrong? ☐☐

12 Do you support your partner in their aspirations for the future? ☐☐

TIER TWO: The decisive areas of compatibility.

This section looks at how much you and your partner have in common, and gauges how the two of you are likely to get on in the future when the early flushes of love have either evaporated or metamorphosed into lasting devotion. It explores 11 major areas of compatibility (or potential friction) and can be instrumental in forecasting the long-term potential of your relationship, even if you have only been together for a few short months or years.

Areas of particular interest in this test include communication/interaction, emotional expression, upbringing, education/interpersonal skills, religious/political/personal views, ambition/needs/children, sex drive/fidelity, work/financial security, shared interests, lifestyle, relaxation and leisure.

All you have to do is indicate the extent to which you agree or disagree with each statement that follows by circling the appropriate response. You must not circle more than one response. You will invalidate the questionnaire if you allow your partner to see your answers before they have completed theirs.

AA = Absolutely agree, A = Agree, N = Neutral/not applicable, D = Disagree,
DD = Definitely disagree

Communication/interaction

13 I feel good when I'm with my partner.　AA A N D DD

14 We enjoy talking with each other.　AA A N D DD

15 My partner makes me laugh.　AA A N D DD

16 I get on well when I am meeting my partner's family and friends.　AA A N D DD

Emotional expression

17 I believe that we bring out the best in each other.　AA A N D DD

18 If my partner accidentally crashed my car, I would be okay about it.　AA A N D DD

19 I sometimes feel intimidated by my partner.　AA A N D DD

20 I have considered the possible
long-term implications and I am
relaxed and comfortable about the
age difference between us.   AA A N D DD

Upbringing

21 My partner's approach to life may be   AA A N D DD
different from mine, but I like it
that way.

22 My partner is from the same   AA A N D DD
ethnic origin and cultural background.

23 I believe in decency and fair play.   AA A N D DD

24 Status is important to me.   AA A N D DD

Education/interpersonal skills

25 I am usually relaxed and comfortable   AA A N D DD
in my partner's company.

26 I regard myself as well educated.   AA A N D DD

27 I believe I have higher than average   AA A N D DD
intelligence.

28 My problem-solving skills are good.   AA A N D DD

Religious/political/personal views/habits

29 I have strong political views.   AA A N D DD

30 I have strong religious/   AA A N D DD
anti-religious views.

31 I can't stand people smoking   AA A N D DD
around me.

32 I take recreational drugs.   AA A N D DD

Ambition/needs/children

33 I believe we are making progress   AA A N D DD
   in anticipating each other's needs.

34 We have shared ambitions for   AA A N D DD
   the future.

35 I find the relationship stimulating   AA A N D DD
   and fulfilling.

36 I would like to have children/   AA A N D DD
   more children.

Sex drive/fidelity

37 My sex drive is insatiable,   AA A N D DD
   I am always up for it.

38 Our sex life is good.   AA A N D DD

39 Regular sex is not a requirement   AA A N D DD
   for me.

40 Sexual fidelity is extremely important   AA A N D DD
   to me.

Work/financial security

41 I value happiness and satisfaction   AA A N D DD
   more highly than money.

42 Financial security is very important   AA A N D DD
   to me.

43 I believe in self-development and   AA A N D DD
   making life better.

44 I enjoy my work/occupation/business/   AA A N D DD
full-time parenting/retirement.

Shared interests
45 I can think of six or more non-sexual   AA A N D DD
activities we enjoy together.

46 We love going out regularly together.   AA A N D DD

47 We share similar values across a range   AA A N D DD
of topics.

48 Family life is very important to me.   AA A N D DD

Lifestyle
49 I am adventurous in my choice of   AA A N D DD
restaurants when eating out.

50 I like to eat chips with most of my   AA A N D DD
hot meals.

51 I like classical music.   AA A N D DD

52 My lifestyle includes good books,   AA A N D DD
films, theatre.

Relaxation and leisure
53 I watch TV for a couple of hours or   AA A N D DD
more several nights each week.

54 I enjoy a few drinks most nights.   AA A N D DD

55 I can't stand football.   AA A N D DD

56 I am willing to accept my partner's   AA A N D DD
choice of holiday destination even
if it doesn't appeal to me.

TIER THREE: The advanced building blocks to a secure and lasting relationship: equilibrium, tolerance, understanding, togetherness and commitment.

Circle the response (only one per question) that seems most appropriate to you and your relationship.

Equilibrium

57 Let's say you had a right royal ding-dong! You've argued, got uptight, let off a lot off steam and the two of you are mad at each other. Afterwards, when you've made up, talked things through rationally, listened to each other's viewpoints and come up with a solution that suits you both, do you feel even closer than you were before?

   a   Always
   b   Often
   c   Seldom
   d   Never
   e   Not applicable – we don't argue

58 Who's getting the best deal out of the relationship?

   a   Me
   b   My partner
   c   Both of us
   d   It's fairly equal
   e   Don't know

Tolerance

59 When your partner is under pressure or stress, are you (or do you think you will be) able to accept him/her at

their worst? (The question assumes that 'their worst'
does not include violence of any kind.)

a Yes
b No
c Maybe

60 Your partner is doing their best, but making a right hash
of some trivial task that you could do far better. Do you:

a Point out the error of their ways?
b Criticise?
c Offer to help?
d Lie back and enjoy the unfolding fiasco?
e Get stuck in and do-it-yourself?

Understanding

61 Do you find it easy to confide in your partner?

a Yes
b No
c Occasionally
d Most of the time

62 In all probability, you and your partner have some
needs, habits, traits, or desires that are not wholly
compatible. Do you:

a Regard yourselves as perfect in every way?
b Try to get your partner to change to suit you?
c Change to suit your partner?
d Work together to bring about a gradual merging of
   compatibility?
e Put your partner's needs before your own occasionally?

Togetherness

63 Looking ahead five years, is there room for your partner in your plans and aspirations?

   a Probably, but I can't be sure because I don't know what the future holds
   b I don't have any plans or aspirations for the future
   c Yes
   d Maybe
   e If all goes according to plan
   f I sincerely hope so

64 Do you share a common view of the relationship, but retain some independence?

   a Yes
   b No
   c Most of the time

Commitment

65 Can you think of anyone that you would rather spend your life with than your partner?

   a Yes
   b No
   c Yes, but this person is not available
   d Don't know
   e I'm not sure

66 If your partner was to fall from grace, would you stand squarely alongside him/her?

a I believe I would
b Except in extreme or unreasonable circumstances, I believe I would
c Probably
e Maybe
f Yes
g Yes, providing my partner hadn't been disloyal to me or acted indecently to anyone else
h No
i This decision must ultimately depend on the reaction of my family, friends, peer group, etc.

Well done! Please let your partner have the completed questionnaire for scoring and then the two of you can work out where you fit in the Matchmaking Equation.

The Bottom Line

This is where you find out if you have what it takes to make a magnificent twosome.

PART 7

Countdown to Love

$$\sum_{n=1}^{20} (X_n + Y_n)^2 = (X_1 + Y_1)^2 + (X_2 + Y_2)^2 + \ldots + (X_{20} + Y_{20})^2 = 100$$

Mathematics possesses not only truth, but also supreme beauty – a beauty cold and austere, like that of a sculpture.

Bertrand Russell
1872–1970

The Countdown

To win, you have to dare to lose.

Willi Railo

The time has come to do the Countdown. This is where you discover the true value of your relationship and whether it has the capacity to last. You have fully answered the questions in Tiers 1 to 3. Your partner has done the same. Now we have to translate your answers into numbers so you can see how you have scored. It is your suitability for each other and the long-term potential of your relationship that we are calculating here, so the scores for each of you on their own have no value. What matters is your joint score and that is why there is only one score sheet between you.

We'll go step-by-step through the point scoring procedure that appears in this, the last chapter, and very soon you will be able to see how your relationship fits in the Matchmaking Equation. What I want you to do now, section by section, tier by tier, is to enter your score on the score sheet that follows.

Please go through your answers and give them numerical scores. As you come to the end of each section in tiers one and three, you will find a section subtotal box. Simply add up the points accumulated in that section only and enter the total in the box.

TIER ONE: The primary building blocks to a secure and lasting relationship

Give yourselves one point between you for each correct answer that both you and your partner got right. If only one of you answered correctly, the score for that question is zero.

Worked example – do not include with your scores!
If you got all three questions right and your partner got questions 1 and 3 right; your scorecard for LUST would look like this:

Lust	Preferred answer/s	You	Your partner	Score
Question 1	yes	yes	yes	1
Question 2	no	no	yes	0
Question 3	yes	yes	yes	1
Section subtotal				2

Now for the real thing.

Lust	Preferred answer/s	You	Your partner	Score
Question 1	yes	....	....	....
Question 2	no	....	....	....
Question 3	yes	....	....	....
Section subtotal				

Friendship	Preferred answer/s	You	Your partner	Score
Question 4	yes	....	....	....
Question 5	yes	....	....	....
Question 6	no	....	....	....
Section subtotal				

Trust	Preferred answer/s	You	Your partner	Score
Question 7	yes	....	....	....
Question 8	yes	....	....	....
Question 9	yes	....	....	....
Section subtotal				

Respect	Preferred answer/s	You	Your partner	Score
Question 10	yes	....	....	....
Question 11	yes	....	....	....
Question 12	yes	....	....	....
Section subtotal				☐

TIER TWO: Compatibility

You have indicated the extent to which you agree or disagree with the statements that appear in 11 different areas of compatibility by circling the appropriate symbol on the reference key. Your partner has done the same. You and your partner jointly score maximum points when all your responses match or almost match in each four-part area of compatibility.

For instance, if your answers match exactly like AA and AA, or are adjacent to each other on the reference key and almost match – say AA and A – you score two points in total for satisfactorily responding to all four statements.

If, on the other hand, any of your responses are two symbols apart on the reference key – for example, A and D or N and DD – you score one point only for that entire area of compatibility.

In the event that even one of your responses is more than two symbols apart – for example, AA and DD or A and DD – your score is zero for all responses throughout that area of compatibility, no matter how well matched your other answers.

To make it easy for you to score correctly, I have listed below all possible combinations of responses, together with their scores. All you need to do is to enter 0, 1 or 2 in the score box for each of the 11 areas of compatibility tested.

Example

Your grading	Your partner's grading	Score
AA	AA	2
A	A	2
N	N	2
D	D	2
DD	DD	2
AA	A	2
A	N	2
N	D	2
D	DD	2
AA	N	1
N	DD	1
A	D	1
AA	DD	0
DD	A	0
AA	D	0

Remember that you score only once for each group of responses, not for each answer.

Communication/interaction
Responses 13–16   SCORE ▷   ◁ 0, 1, or 2

Emotional expression
Responses 17–20   SCORE ▷   ◁ 0, 1, or 2

Upbringing
Responses 21–24   SCORE ▷   ◁ 0, 1, or 2

Education/interpersonal skills
Responses 25–28   SCORE ▷   ◁ 0, 1, or 2

Religious/political/personal views
Responses 29–32   SCORE ▷   ◁ 0, 1, or 2

Ambition/needs/children		
Responses 33 – 36	SCORE ◊	◊ 0, 1, or 2
Sex drive/fidelity		
Responses 37 – 40	SCORE ◊	◊ 0, 1, or 2
Work/financial security		
Responses 41 – 44	SCORE ◊	◊ 0, 1, or 2
Shared interests		
Responses 45 – 48	SCORE ◊	◊ 0, 1, or 2
Lifestyle		
Responses 49 – 52	SCORE ◊	◊ 0, 1, or 2
Relaxation and leisure		
Responses 53 – 56	SCORE ◊	◊ 0, 1, or 2

Well done! That's the marathon out of the way and there's no need to add your points together just yet. Let's get straight on with marking tier three because it won't be long now before you discover the value of your relationship and how it stacks up against the Matchmaking Equation.

TIER THREE: The advanced building blocks to a secure and lasting relationship.

This test consists of five sections with two questions in each. One point per couple is scored when both parties select an option that scores – even if the answer chosen from the option list turns to be different from your partner's. Naturally, no score results from any question when either or both parties choose a non-scoring answer.

Please go through your answers and give them number scores in points. As you come to the end of each section, you will find a section subtotal box. Simply add up the points accumulated in that section only and enter the total in the box.

Worked example

If you got both questions right but your partner selected option e for question 57 and option a for question 58 (although you selected option c), your scorecard for Equilibrium would look like this:

Equilibrium	Preferred answer/s	You	Your partner	Score
Question 57	a	✓	✗	0
Question 58	a, c, d	✓	✓	1
Section subtotal				1

Now for the real thing again.

Equilibrium	Preferred answer/s	You	Your partner	Score
Question 57	a	....	....	
Question 58	a, c, d	....	....	
Section subtotal				☐

Tolerance	Preferred answer/s	You	Your partner	Score
Question 59	a	....	....	....
Question 60	c, d, e	....	....	....
Section subtotal				☐

Understanding	Preferred answer/s	You	Your partner	Score
Question 61	a, d	....	....	....
Question 62	d, e	....	....	....
Section subtotal				☐

Togetherness	Preferred answer/s	You	Your partner	Score
Question 63	c, f	....	....	....
Question 64	a, c	....	....	....
Section subtotal				☐

Commitment	Preferred answer/s	You	Your partner	Score
Question 65	b	....	....	....
Question 66	a, b, e, f	....	....	....
Section subtotal				☐

Congratulations on completing the marking element of the questionnaires. You are very close to completing the equation and finding out whether or not you and your partner are ideally suited to each other for a long-term relationship.

Now is the time to transfer each of your subtotals from the 20 different sections tested throughout tiers 1, 2 and 3 to the first column marked A on the chart that follows.

So far, so good, but we need to do a little bit of elementary mathematics to square your result with the equation. This is necessary because the power of multiplication fast-forwards the impact you and your partner will have on each other in the future. What you write in column B, the central box on the chart that follows, will depend on what you put in column A. The calculation is easy because the only possible result you could have scored and entered in column A is zero, one, two or three.

If your score in column A was zero, put 0 in column B.
If your score in column A was one, put 1 in column B.
If your score in column A was two, put 4 in column B.
If your score in column A was three, put 9 in column B.

Next, add up your column B scores for each tier and put the total in box C.

All that remains to be done now is to add together your column C totals for tiers 1, 2 and 3 and insert the grand total at the bottom of the chart marked Add scores in column C to arrive at the grand total for the equation.

The Matchmaking Equation joint score sheet

		A score	B score	C totals
Tier 1				
1–3	Lust	1	1	
4–6	Friendship	3	9	
7–9	Trust	2	4	
10–12	Respect	2	4	
	Total for tier 1B (only) ◊			18
Tier 2				
13–16	Communication/interaction	2	4	
17–20	Emotional expression	2	4	
21–24	Upbringing	2	4	
25–28	Education/interpersonal skills	1	1	
29–32	Religious/political/personal views/habits	1	1	
33–36	Ambition/needs/children	1	1	
37–40	Sex drive/fidelity	1	1	
41–44	Work/financial security		1	
45–48	Shared interests	1	1	
49–52	Lifestyle	2	4	
53–56	Relaxation and leisure	2	4	
	Total for tier 2B (only) ◊			26
Tier 3				
57–58	Equilibrium	1	1	
59–60	Tolerance	1	1	
61–62	Understanding	2	4	
63–64	Togetherness	2	4	
65–66	Commitment	0	0	
	Total for tier 3B (only) ◊			10

Add scores in column C to
arrive at the grand total for the equation ◊ 44
54

Your grand total now registers as an exact percentage of 100 per cent – the full value of the Matchmaking Equation. What does this mean for your chances of happiness and fulfilment with your partner and the long-term success of your relationship? Now that we have all the figures to hand, let's refer to the Countdown!

100%	You've been cheating! If not, congratulations – you have a relationship to die for! Each of you has every right to feel proud because you are already, or will almost certainly become, a magnificent twosome.
90–99%	Excellent.
80–89%	Very promising.
70–79%	Promising, but you need to look at the areas where you are not connecting with each other.
60–69%	Rocky. You must identify the issues that divide you and bridge the gaps.
50–59%	Risky. Could be rescued, but there are significant problems to be addressed.
Below 50%	Find a new partner! Remember that the divorce rate in many western countries is higher than your score.

I hope the journey through the book has been interesting and eventful for you. If you have scored high in the Countdown, we wish you every happiness and success for the future and bid you farewell. If magnificent twosomeness is your objective but you haven't got there yet, remember that we run a series of love and relationship seminars and workshops and should you come to one of them – alone or with your partner – we hope you will make yourself known to us.

Good luck!

 The Bottom Line

It's your call!

Postscript

Emboldened by the depth of our love for each other, Tatiana and I, as a mathematician and a writer, felt that we had a contribution to make to the problem of finding the right partner and enjoying a lifelong relationship together. We would be delighted to hear from readers who have benefited from this book and you can contact us by writing to David and Tatiana Hinds, c/o Foulsham, The Publishing House, Bennetts Close, Slough SL1 5AP, UK.

If you would like to explore further how to find Mr or Ms Absolutely Right, you can do so in an environment where virtually every person you meet is genuinely looking for a lasting relationship with the right partner. Tatiana and I are currently hosting a series of Countdown weekend seminars, meeting opportunities and relationship workshops in major cities across the country. They are open exclusively to *Countdown to Love* readers and seminar participants. This ensures that everyone taking part has a commitment to finding a meaningful relationship, or elevating an existing one to magnificent twosome status.

You can find out more and book tickets for these venues by calling the Countdown box office on 0870 609 4096 or by visiting www.countdowntolove.com.

Index